D0113608

Caring For Your Parents
When The Golden Years Fade

Anita Johnson

COLLEGE PRESS PUBLISHING COMPANY • JOPLIN, MISSOURI

Library of Congress Cataloging-in-Publication Data

Johnson, Anita, 1934–
    Sunset decisions: caring for your parents when the golden
years fade / Anita Johnson
        p. cm.
    ISBN 0-89900-811-9 (pbk.)
    1. Aging parents—Care—United States. 2. Adult children—
United States—Family relationships. 3. Adult children—
United States—Psychology. I. Title.
HQ1064.U5J637 1998
306.874—dc21   98-9947
                                                         CIP

TABLE OF CONTENTS

Introduction

Not at my best at three a.m., I was struggling to put some "paper underwear" on my invalid mother while she was lying in bed. She was giving me all the help she could but her weakness combined with my clumsiness made the job difficult. Finally, it was on, but crooked. To straighten it, I gave it a good tug. With a soft, swishing sound, it tore in half. Furious, I ripped it off, flung it on the floor and said, "d——, d——, d——". Horrors! I had just cussed in front of my sweet, little Christian mother. I timidly stole a glance at her. She lay there shaking and almost choking. I realized she was laughing so hard she could hardly catch her breath.

For my mother, growing old hadn't given her many reasons to laugh. It hadn't been much fun. Mother's mind remained good but her body ceased to serve her. A few years earlier, my father's mind was impaired while his body remained healthy. So much for growing old with dignity.

For fifteen years I was, on some level, a caregiver. It was during those challenging years this book was born.

ENCOURAGEMENT AND OPTIONS

I want this book to provide you with two things, **ENCOURAGEMENT** for you as you face the burden of aging, either of yourself or a parent, and information regarding the **OPTIONS** which are available to you.

If you have picked up this book, you are probably a caregiver. There are more and more of us all the time. Most people between the age of 40 to 60 years are providing some care or help to a parent. In fact we read that more work days are lost by people providing elder care than child care.

7

Introduction

I will share with you my story and the stories of many of my friends and acquaintances who are caregivers. I have been thrilled with some of the creative ways people are finding to meet the needs of elderly parents. I want to tell you some of the things we have done right. I want you to profit from the mistakes we have made. Most of all I want to offer you what we have learned.

You need to know what **options** are available to you. You need to know why moving a parent out of their home may be a big mistake. You need to know what other options there are for the parent who has difficulty living alone. You need to know how to choose a nursing home and when. You need to know how to recognize when your parent's mind is going. You need to know what resources are available to you for help and guidance. I will tell you about Elder Care experts who are available to you as well as refer you to research which has been done by agencies like Consumer Reports.

I have used the terms "children" and "parents," fully aware that there are wonderful people who provide care and help for people who may be only distantly related if they are related at all. I know a couple who looked after the husband's elderly cousin who had no nearer relatives. They found a good nursing home for her and visited and monitored her care. I have neighbors, Bob and Lois, who looked after her elderly aunt until she died. God has a special crown for those who care for elderly people who haven't the claim which our parents have on us for help.

My prayer for you is for **WISDOM** as you walk this delicate tightrope of maintaining your parent's dignity and happiness by keeping their life as intact as possible, and at the same time provide for their basic needs; **PEACE** as you deal with less than perfect and often very temporary solutions; and **STRENGTH** as you balance your roles as a caregiver, spouse, parent, grandparent, worker, sibling and friend. To that end, this book is dedicated.

1 | Too Much Too Soon

"A wise son brings joy to his father,
but a foolish son grief to his mother."
Proverbs 10:1 (NIV)

If I only accomplish one thing with this book, I hope it will be to prevent loving children from uprooting parents from their homes when it isn't necessary. Too many times the desire to rescue and fix a parent's life causes children to take from the parent one of the most important things they have left, the comfort of living in their own home. To illustrate, I will tell you two stories.

THE KELLER FAMILY

Julie Keller was my neighbor when we lived in California. About ten years ago, her father-in law died suddenly. The shocked and grieving family rushed to Mother Keller's side. After the funeral, the children and Mother Keller's youngest sister had a conference regarding how to best care for eighty-five year old Mother Keller. The family agreed that she shouldn't stay in her big house in her small town in Arkansas when her four children lived at the four corners of the United States.

Then Sister Sally suggested that she would like for Mother Keller to come live with her in Florida. The fact that Mother Keller's oldest daughter, Mary, lives in a town nearby was added incentive for the family to move Mother Keller to Sister Sally's home. The family wanted Mother Keller out of her big house, in milder winters, near one of her children, not living alone. The advantages seemed clear and those advantages blinded the loving family to the things Mother Keller would lose by a move.

Too Much Too Soon

While mom was still numb from losing her husband, the house was put on the market, all but a few personal possessions were placed with an estate sale agency, and mom was packed off to live with Sister Sally.

A few months later mom came out of her "fog" and realized that she had no friends, no home, in fact, no life. It has been ten years now. Julie says Mother Keller and Sally get along fine but shy Mother Keller hasn't made any friends. Sally, long established in the community, has her own circle of friends and her own activities. Sally is willing to include Mother Keller in her activities, but Mother Keller plays neither bridge nor golf. Additionally, she feels out of place as a tagalong with her sister.

Sister Sally travels a great deal. Having Mother Keller to look after the house and pets while she is away is ideal for Sally. But this leaves mom home alone in a neighborhood where she knows no one, in fact feels isolated and afraid. Mother Keller doesn't drive and no stores are within walking distance.

Mary is generous with her help but everything mom needs, trips to the store, church, beauty shop, and doctors, take up a lot of time. Mary has her own family and life so by the time she does the necessary things for mom, there is little time to do fun things together.

A loving family made the wrong decision at the wrong time for their mother.

Recap: Let's look back on what mom had before. A big house which was a lot of work, but full of her things and her memories. Additionally, that big house was in a small town where Mother Keller knew everyone. She could walk to the store and beauty shop. Longtime friends were happy to pick her up for church and take her to the "Authorized" restaurant where most of the older members ate Sunday dinner. It is true the winters brought snow and ice storms, but with a little planning, mom could "hole up" during the worst of the storms and the local grocery store would deliver to the senior citizens who were regular customers.

Best of all, what mom had, in her hometown, was her "LIFE." The very real concerns of her children needed to be considered, but they did too much, too soon. We will deal in another chapter about looking, one by one, at the concerns and problems which a family has about the older parent who is living alone, and then solving each problem individually rather than sweeping changes.

The next story is about a family who had even more reason to move a parent. Moving the father was a hard decision made over a longer period of time after other solutions had been tried. But as you can see the results were still tragic.

THE EVANS FAMILY

Shirley Evans has been my friend for many years so I shared with her the difficulty the family experienced as they tried first to support Father Evans in his home and then as they agonized over how best to care for him. With her permission, I will tell you her family's story.

Shirley's father-in-law, Howard, lived in Wisconsin. He lived alone with his little dog. Shirley is married to Fred, Howard's only son. On her frequent visits to Wisconsin, Shirley spent time with Howard. Gradually she could see that the aging process, added to his tendency to imbibe frequent beers, were taking its toll on Howard's ability to care for his home as well as himself. A visit to Howard sent Shirley into a flurry of cleaning, washing and ironing. She would also take the dog to a veterinarian to rid him of fleas and update his shots.

Naturally, her semiannual cleanings didn't have lasting effect, and the next visit showed the house, the dog and Howard dirtier than ever.

This went on for a long time as Shirley searched for a solution. She contacted various social and health care agencies. At one time it was arranged for someone to come in on a regular basis to bathe Howard and clean up the house. Howard refused to have this done.

Shirley considered their moving back to Wisconsin where they could look after Howard. But Fred had a business in California and their three children were in school. Moving to Wisconsin didn't seem to be a good solution. They asked Howard to move close to them in California. He refused.

11

Various services for the elderly were tried but Howard's lack of cooperation if not downright opposition, made all attempts unsuccessful. Additionally, the social agencies were pressuring the family to take better care of Howard. They just didn't explain how this was to be done.

After one visit, Shirley said the house was getting so bad that she felt that the health department would condemn it if any of the social agencies reported the conditions. I questioned her closely about that statement, pointing out that there were times when our children's rooms were so bad we claimed the health department might condemn *our* houses. Her reply was, "Trust me, Howard's house is no joke, it really *is* a filthy pig pen. There are dirty dishes, rotten food and the bathroom . . . I won't even try to describe. No self-respecting cleaning woman would touch it at this point."

The one favorable factor was that Howard had a good friend, Earl, who came by each day. He brought Howard groceries, made sure all was well and stayed to drink beer and talk. This relieved Shirley and Fred of the concern that Howard might be ill or injured and no one would know.

Gratefully, they began to pay Earl for extra tasks. Earl was successful in getting Howard to bathe and change clothes occasionally. He maintained the furnace during the winter and made sure bills were paid. Then Earl dropped dead with a heart attack.

At this point, it seemed impossible to allow Howard to remain in his home. Shirley and Fred decided that the best choice would be to bring him to live with them in California. They added rooms to their house to relieve crowding and then brought Howard for a "visit." With true sweetness, Shirley even brought his elderly dog.

From that point on, nothing went well. Howard was miserable at Shirley and Fred's house. His only thought was to get back home. He became very adept at running away.

The dear little doggie, too, didn't seem to appreciate his clean, flea-free surroundings. He forgot his toilet training, fought with the children's dog, and finally reverted to biting anyone, except Howard, who touched him.

Howard's frequent, successful escapes from their home frightened Shirley and Fred so much, they decided to place him in a secure care facility. No dogs were allowed in the secure facility, no beer as well.

For the rest of his life, Howard had not one happy moment. He had lost his dog, his friend, his home and his beer. True, he was clean, his surroundings were clean and he was fed well. But he lived a prisoner not only in his surroundings but in his mind. Soon he didn't even know his son and visits to their home gave him no pleasure.

"And for what?" Shirley asked. "What had seemed so vital to us, mattered not at all to Howard. What we offered him, a home with his family, clean surroundings and all the amenities of a well run home were not what mattered to him. He was better off in his own home with the dirt. He might have died of bad food, but would that have been worse than dying of a broken heart?"

The sad but important moral of this story is this: What you want for your parent may not be what they want for themselves. This is important to remember. What we want for them may seem to be so right. It may seem that they will enjoy the wonderful things we want to give and do for them. But it is *so* hard to judge how well they will function outside familiar surroundings.

This is where we need to be clear about what we want to accomplish. At what cost to the parent are we willing to extend their life?

Was the risk to Howard's life from unsanitary living conditions worse than his losing the things he loved most? Even though I am well aware that it is not possible in all cases to let the parent decide how and where they should live, the big danger is that what *we* want to fix, may not be what *they* want fixed.

This was certainly a hard call. Shirley states that she is sorry they ever moved Howard from his home, but even with hindsight it is hard to see how Howard could have been left in his own home. It is still helpful to consider what Howard had. He had his own home where he could function in a familiar place.

He had the companionship of his little dog. He had his beer. In short he had what he really wanted most.

It had seemed that sanitary conditions might lengthen his life. In reality, the move probably shortened his life. Additionally, the quality of his life in terms of what he wanted was destroyed.

I don't tell these two stories to condemn or criticize either family. Only to show the danger of, in the first case moving too fast, and in the second case . . . perhaps to emphasize how tragic moving a parent can be.

In the next chapter, we will attempt to show alternative solutions to the problems a family faces in providing help to a parent who is growing older.

2 | Patch, Patch

A simple man believes anything,
but a prudent man gives thought to his steps.
Proverbs 14:15 NIV

One of the most important resources you can tap into as a caregiver is the ability to look at the problems your parent may be facing one item at a time. Otherwise you will just see a big gaping hole of need and do "Too much, Too soon," rather than meeting the true needs of the parent. This is a little like throwing away a good garment only because it needs a little mending.

Let me illustrate with the Keller family story. First, we all know, but it is easy to forget, that immediately after the death of a loved one is a terrible time to make major, lasting changes. That was the first mistake the Keller family made.

Additionally, this grief-stricken family was eager to rescue their mother from what looked like a **big problem** which called for **big solutions**. They looked at Mother Keller, suddenly left alone, and saw a joyless, lonely existence ahead for her. They pictured her burdened by her big house, facing hard, cold winters. That picture, expanded, probably had her slipping and falling on an icy sidewalk, breaking a hip. Or, worse yet, falling in the tub and lying injured for days before anyone discovered her. I can relate to their fears because even when my mother lived just ten minutes away, my worst fear was that she would be injured and not be able to summon help.

Visits from her children were a big problem since she lived so far from a major airport. Her daughter-in-law, Julie, told me that they had to fly from California to Dallas/Fort Worth Airport then take a feeder flight to Fayetteville, Arkansas. (The feeder flight was always on the furthest side of the airport and there was never enough time to comfortably get there.) Even when they arrived in Fayetteville, they still were not at their destination. At that point, the two transportation choices were either mule train or pack horse into the remote wiles of the Ozarks. This is Julie's story. I repeat it just as she told it to me.

Grief-stricken, burdened, lonely, vulnerable, remote — it was a picture which broke their hearts.

Let's turn the clock back ten years and take the picture apart one problem at a time to see if we can come up with some better solutions than moving Mother Keller to Florida.

GRIEF-STRICKEN

The first problem and most immediate one is that Mother Keller has just lost her husband. Naturally the family doesn't want to return to their homes and leave her alone with her grief, without providing some kind of support system for her.

The first thing a caregiver must do with a parent who is still mentally clear, is to **ask them what they want.** Mother Keller is in no position to decide on long range plans on the day of her husband's funeral, but she has some feelings about where she wants to be. It is important to ask.

Let us assume for a moment that Mother Keller has no answers. Then the family must look at the immediate problem and make a plan which is *temporary*. I can't stress *temporary* enough. The more flexibility you can maintain to any change made to a parent's life, the easier it will be to correct mistakes which will inevitably be made.

OPTIONS

Let's look at some options. (1) Mother Keller might go for a *visit* to Sister Sally's. OR (2) She might like to visit one of her children. My guess is that if asked, Mother Keller would choose to stay home. There is something about losing a loved one, especially a spouse, which makes one want to be in their own home around familiar things.

16

The "stay at home" option might look like this. (Remember we are talking about temporary solutions.) Sally or one of the children might be able to remain for a few weeks. Or one of the grandchildren might be able to stay for a while. (Of course we are not talking about very young grandchildren.) Or there may be a close friend or family member in the community who could stay for a few days, if Mother Keller agreed. At the very least, the family might find someone who would agree to come on a daily basis for an agreed period of time. Mother Keller's Ladies Bible Class might rotate visits, keeping in mind that the first few days or weeks Mother Keller will be numb. The pain starts later just about the time friends are beginning to stop visiting so often.

Whatever solutions can be found, nothing permanent should be attempted until Mother Keller begins to feel like herself again.

BURDENED

Next let's look at the big house problem. Julie told me that since Mother Keller was in her mid-eighties when Father Keller died, the family felt sure she was getting too old to care for her large house. (At this writing, Mother Keller is in her mid-nineties and still strong and active.) It is true that she no longer has Dad Keller to put up storm windows and do things around the yard. But people can be hired to do those things. And rooms can be shut off so they are not heated or cleaned. Later, when she is feeling better, the big house may be an advantage. She may find a friend or acceptable person to share the house with her. (See the item on shared housing.)

LONELY

There is no way in which a woman who has just lost her husband will not experience loneliness. Dad Keller's death will have left a hole in her life which she can never fill. This doesn't mean, however, that she will never enjoy her life again. If Mother Keller had been permitted to remain in her hometown she would have had her old friends from her church and community to provide companionship. She would have been less lonely in her hometown.

VULNERABLE

Surveillance is the answer to this concern the family has for Mother Keller. Surveillance in the form of regular visits and phone calls from friends or local family members who will agree to do this. Also, even small towns in Arkansas have "lifelines" or monitors which an elderly person can wear in case they "fall and can't get up." And with four children, even at the four corners of the United States, Mother Keller should receive four phone calls a week, each on a different day.

Additionally, Mother Keller's children should counsel her regarding people who prey on elderly people, feeding their fears in order to extort money from them. This should be done in a very tactful way to avoid seeming to say that Mother Keller is dumb and may be taken in. My own mother's response to my suggesting that she could expect calls from people who wanted to take advantage of her newly widowed status, was a scathing look and a contemptuous, "Do you think I was born yesterday?" A smart lady was my mother.

REMOTE

Mother Keller's small town in Arkansas was remote in terms of reaching her by air. Mother Keller's children found it difficult to visit. Either a long automobile trip or a costly and cumbersome combo air trip, rent-a-car was the only way of visiting. Having a parent living in an area where it is difficult to visit is a valid concern. Mother Keller's children knew that she would enjoy and benefit from frequent visits from her children and they added that to their reasons for moving her. But like any other change to her life, that had to be weighed against what she lost in the move.

Keep in mind that most things are temporary. In fact, the son in California (Julie's husband), within a year of his father's death, took a job in Wichita, Kansas. This move was unforeseen. But it placed him within a few hours' drive from Northwest Arkansas, and Mother Keller's hometown. But, of course, by then she was in Florida.

Usually when children move a parent because they are far away, it is for the children's convenience. I don't mean for that statement to sound cruel. Of course the child wants the parent nearer so that they can see the parent more, and do more for the parent. But the losses for the parent may outweigh the benefits.

SUMMATION

The key to making good decisions and avoiding painful mistakes are as follows: Find out what the parent wants to do. Whenever possible, avoid major changes and when major changes are made, stay flexible. Identify the problem(s). Try to find a solution to each problem without tearing the fabric of the parent(s) life apart. (This often means allowing them to remain in their own home.) In other words patch, patch.

3 | Success Stories

"Children's children are a crown to the aged,
and parents are the pride of their children,
Proverbs 17:6 NIV

There are times when moving a parent from their home is the right thing to do. I don't want to leave the impression that in every case this is a mistake. Sometimes the move option is not only best but can be, under some circumstances, happily successful. I will share with you two stories where elderly people moved and were glad they made the move. Then, I will try to show just why I believe these two moves were successful.

SHANNON STORY:

His name is Joseph Shannon. I met him recently when his proud daughter brought him to our house to show him the Hill Country west of Austin and offer him a swim in our pool. Actually she brought him out to show him off because she is terribly proud of him. And well she might be, for at 93 he is straight, handsome and truly delightful.

His mind is clear and he hasn't lost his zest for life. He was interested in our garden, our grandchildren and us. He declined using the pool because his hip was *a little stiff.*

Mr. Shannon lived until last year, near Ft. Worth, Texas. He lived alone in a little house right across the road from a restaurant where each day he ate his main meal. Then the road was converted to a major highway with no safe pedestrian crossing and he could no longer walk to his restaurant. That, combined with his children's concern that he needed to live near them, prompted his son and daughter, both living in Austin, to suggest that Mr. Shannon move to Austin. Harold, the son, found an apartment near his house with the added bonus that the manager was willing to cook a good meal each day for Mr. Shannon.

Mr. Shannon willingly agreed to the move and when he visited us, he was nicely settled in. The manager cooked just the kind of meals he liked, and better yet, she had a cute little granddaughter who was a frequent visitor.

He has made friends in the apartment complex, attends and enjoys church, fishes with his son and goes by airplane to visit his other son in Denver.

Why has this all been so successful? Largely, of course, because Mr. Shannon is still in very good health, both physically and mentally. Additionally, his flexible, outward looking attitude has helped him make friends. Another thing in his favor is that two of his favorite hobbies, whittling and fishing, were "transferable" to Austin. Possibly the biggest thing in making the move successful is that his residence near Ft. Worth was not his "family" home with a lifetime of memories and friends to leave behind. He did have some nieces and nephews in Ft. Worth whom he misses but being near two of his children greatly compensates for not having them around and his son takes him back to visit them occasionally.

Additionally, being a man was in his favor. Women are generally "nest builders." A woman's home takes on special meaning. Her possessions can be an extension of who she is and what her life is all about. It is often easier to transplant fathers than mothers into a new place.

Finally I would point out that he was amenable to the move and he is still living independently. Although the manager is providing daily surveillance and a good meal, he is still in his own place not living with his son. His dignity and privacy are maintained.

It certainly is possible to move a parent, and that often is a good thing to do. It is just hard to have all the ducks in a row, as happened in the case of Mr. Shannon. A key question to ask is, "What will the parent give up, and what will be gained from the move?"

MOM'S STORY:

My mother, Gladys Tarbet, lost my sweet stepfather when she was 75 years old. Her physical strength was waning (not just from being 75 but from small T.I.A.'s she was having). However, she was strong enough to walk to the store and work in her garden. My brother, Gene, lived a few blocks away and I lived ten minutes away. So, naturally, we didn't anticipate her having to move from her home.

As time went by she didn't wish to be alone in her house. She was afraid as well as lonely. Her solution was to find a young man to "rent" her front bedroom and bath. During the next two years she had two nice young men (one at a time) share her home. By the time the last one moved out, mother didn't try to find another "house mate." She had grown weaker and had very poor balance. She had given up gardening. She could no longer walk the three blocks to the grocery store or her beauty shop.

Almost everything she had to do from preparing a simple meal to taking out the trash was a challenge. We arranged for Meals on Wheels which solved part of her problem. But the bottom line was that mother could no longer maintain her house. My brother and I tried to help as much as we could but each of us had our own businesses and homes to maintain so the amount of time we could spend in maintaining mother's home was limited. Mother didn't want to hire someone to clean. Besides she needed more than a cleaning person, she needed a maid. Finally mother realized that her home had become more of a burden than a joy.

She was aware of the numerous Retirement Hotels in our area but she had two concerns. First, she had a little dog which she didn't want to give up, and second, she was wasn't sure she could afford the rent at a Retirement Hotel. If my memory serves, in 1985 in Orange County, California the rent for a room in a brand new retirement hotel was $900.00 per month.

One day she got a call from a new retirement facility called "Bradford Square." The director invited her to come for lunch and look around. Mom brought up the problem of the little dog. The director said that some dogs would be accepted.

There were downstairs rooms which opened into gardens where a dog could be walked.

The day we visited we were all on our best behavior, including the dog. Bradford was truly lovely. The rooms were large enough for a bedroom and small sitting area. Mom fell in love with the burgundy and dusty rose colors. She could furnish her room with her own things or the facility had set pieces they would furnish.

There was no kitchen area in the room we considered, but mother said if she never again had to prepare even a snack, that would be fine with her. Also, there was a beauty shop on the premises for her weekly shampoo and set. Bradford had subtle little touches like handrails along the corridors for little ladies who might lose their balance and benches and chairs where one could sit for a moment.

Mother was sold. The only problem left was the cost which seemed enormous to mom. To put the cost into perspective for her, we sat down and listed what it cost mother to live in her own house. We added up gardening, utilities and food. Gene, who was in real-estate, said he could get her $700.00 a month in rent for her house so we added that amount to her "stay at home" cost.

Then we showed her what her income would be if she let Gene rent her house. (If renting had not been an option, we would have estimated the income she could expect from selling the house and carefully investing the money.) The rent plus her other income was enough to pay the rent at the retirement hotel with some left over for personal care, telephone and an estimated maintenance cost on her house. Financially, it looked like a break even.

Gene and I had some concerns about how well mother would adjust. Mother was friendly but made few real friends. She had never been a joiner and didn't enjoy playing games of any kind. We need not have worried. She "joined" the exercise group which met four mornings to do exercises appropriate for elderly people. She attended the once a week book reviews given by someone from the local library. She attended the fashion shows put on by local dress shops. When a special movie was shown in the television room, she was there. In fact she was rarely in her room. She found many of the other residents very interesting and enjoyed their stories. She loved the food and began benefiting from a better diet. I think, most of all she enjoyed the attention she received from the well-trained staff.

She even became more outgoing with friends at church. She was happy to have them drop by because she was proud of her living quarters. The message she could send by living in such a lovely, active place was, "I have come here to enjoy the security and convenience of this place, not because I am ill and need a place to die."

The first and only hitch came early on. The dog, who had never been properly "potty trained," became a problem for her. In her own house, with a doggie door, she had not noticed that the dog frequently urinated in the house. In her much smaller living area, she realized that the dog was using her lovely drapes as a fire hydrant. She didn't want her room ruined nor did she want to ruin someone else's property. She called me during the first week and wept with frustration. I reminded her that her house was still empty and she could move back in at any time she wanted to. It turned out that she loved Bradford so much that she couldn't bear to leave. She was willing to give up the dog if we could find it a good home.

We all hated the dog who didn't hesitate to bite anyone who displeased him, but I brought him to my house on a temporary basis while the entire family tried to find a home for an **"non-house-trained, sixteen-year-old dog who hates children."** I will carry the secret of how we solved that problem to my grave.

WHY IT WORKED:

The most important reason the move was good for my mom was that she had an opportunity to try everything else. She had successfully extended her stay in her own home by sharing her home for two years. Finally, she had reached the decision, on her own, that living in her own home was more of a burden than a joy. After trying the retirement living, she was sold. But her willingness to even try it was based on two things. First, if she had hated it, she wasn't locked in to anything. She still had her house to move back to. And her rent at the retirement home was month to month so she knew she could move out any time she wasn't happy there. She wasn't locked in financially. I believe even if she hadn't liked Bradford Square, she would have tried another retirement place. Second, their willingness to take her pet removed a major obstacle.

She, like Mr. Shannon, was not emotionally tied to her house or neighborhood. Being married to a preacher, she had moved several times. She was able to take with her the personal mementos which she treasured.

Having experienced loneliness, she was prepared to appreciate the company which Bradford supplied. Having reached the point where even light housework was a burden, she appreciated the daily maid service.

Mom actually became more outgoing and happy after the move. So moving a parent under some circumstances can be a positive change, relieving both the parent and caregivers of many worrisome burdens. To assist in determining what will be lost and what will be gained for the parent by a move, I am submitting a list of questions which you may find helpful.

I suggest that not only should the parent(s) answer the questions, but each of their children answer as they think the parent might. This should be a good basis for a family meeting (see chapter 11)

Gains andLosses

What is the biggest problem in remaining at home?
What are some other problems in remaining at home?
Has your home become more of a burden than a joy?
What are your favorite activities?
Can you do them in the place to which you are considering moving?
What is it costing you to live at home?
  (add the amount you could receive as
  rent or other income if you sold your house
  and the money was wisely invested.)

What do you think you would give up by moving from
　　your house?
What would you gain by moving?
Who would you miss by moving?
Who might you see more?

　You may want to add questions of your own. This should be
good information in helping the family come to a decision.
Remember the key: **what would be lost**, and **what would be
gained.**

4 | Stay at Home Living Options

From there, David went to Mizpah in Moab and said to the king of Moab, "Would you let my father and mother come and stay with you until I learn what God will do for me?" So he left them with the king of Moab, and they stayed with him as long as David was in the stronghold.
1 Samuel 22:3-5 NIV

It is interesting that three thousand years ago David found a creative way of having his parents cared for. He surely had few options. Up until a few years ago in this country, most elderly people had few options if they could no longer live alone. They could move in with one of their children or go to a nursing home. The very wealthy, of course, could live in nice hotels like the Waldorf Astoria, with daily maid service, room service and many other services on the premises.

Thankfully, there are many options now even for the not so rich. In the following chapters, we will try to list as many options as I am aware of and share with you true stories about how these seem to work.

AT HOME ASSISTANCE

The first option to be considered, as mentioned in chapter two, is to look at ways of maintaining or supporting an elderly person in their own home. This assumes that, first, the elderly person has no dementia and, second, that remaining in his own home is his wish. There are many good reasons for supporting a parent's wish to remain in her own home. Aside from the fact she may be happier in her own home, it is likely the most economical way for her to live even with the extra help which must be paid for as she becomes less able to care for house and yard. More compelling than the economic reason are those cases where both parents are living and one parent is physically disabled or developing dementia. This, also, becomes the most demanding level of support when the family must provide for two elderly parents, the caregiver and the disabled one. But two people who have been married for years should not be separated because one needs nursing care which the spouse is unable to provide.

Maintaining a parent(s) in their own home usually requires a commitment from willing family and friends, a willingness to pay for some or many services and tapping into community resources. (One resourceful lady got free at-home assistance for her mother through various local, state and federal agencies totaling thirty hours a week!)

I think you will see from the stories that follow that there are many ways families have found to meet this challenge.

SURVEILLANCE

When a parent is living alone, usually the family's first concern is surveillance. What if the elderly person falls or becomes ill and can't summon help? One solution is the "lifeline." Another could be daily calls from family and friends. Fortunate is the elderly person who has solicitous neighbors. I used to call mom at home each day. If I didn't get an answer, I would wait one half hour and call again. If I didn't get an answer, I would call my brother whose office was five minutes from her house. He would "drop by" for a short visit.

Thirty years ago, when my grandmother was living alone, she not only needed surveillance because of a faulty heart valve but was afraid to be alone. She didn't want to move away from her house and her friends in the neighborhood. Her little house was too small for her to share or hire a live-in, but her little house sat on the back of a large city lot zoned R-2. My aunt Mary and uncle Joe sold their large home and moved a compact house to the front of grandmother's property. Uncle Joe rigged a buzzer system so grandmother could summon them if she felt unwell. Theirs was the first example I observed of a creative solution to maintaining a parent in their own home. Grandmother was able to take care of her personal needs and remained at home until her death at age 93.

SAFETY

There are several ways of making an elderly person safer in their own home. There are the obvious things like good handrails wherever there are steps, grab bars in the bathroom and shower, non-skid things for the bathtub, and smoke detectors. Look through an AARP catalogue, walk through a hospital supply store or a pharmacy that sells things for handicapped people. There are all kinds of useful gadgets for older people which most of us never dreamed of.

Do the same thing you did when your children were toddlers; walk through the house looking for problem areas. Are there rugs which might be tripped over? Some older people collect and stack a lot of stuff. Perhaps they will let you move some things to the attic, basement or garage so areas where they need to walk are clear.

Post by their phone the 911 number in **LARGE** numbers. If they are able to learn to use rapid dial numbers, a telephone which is set up with all the frequently called numbers on instant dial can save them valuable time during an emergency.

Make sure they understand that good manners does not require them to open their door to anyone whom they don't know. Their front door should have a peephole at the correct height so they can look outside to see who is ringing their bell without opening the door. Find a neighbor who will agree to come over if the elderly person is unsure about who may want to come into their house. If someone asks to use the phone and the elderly person can refer them to the family next door they will be less likely to let their kind heart overcome their good judgment.

NOURISHING MEALS

Making sure the elderly person has at least one good meal a day is very important. As my mother's energy waned, we realized she was less able to shop for and prepare nourishing meals. We realized she was eating only easy things. Additionally, some medications will diminish the appetite. Some will make the tummy a little queasy so the older person will reach for mild foods like ice cream and puddings. You should ask the doctor or pharmacist about what effect your parents' medications might have on their appetite. Nutrition has a profound effect on anyone, especially elderly people, so good meals are a priority.

Until recently, a friend of mine, Helen drove to her mother's house in east Texas every three weeks. She shopped, cooked, and froze meals. Recently Helen has found an acceptable person to come in and do the cooking for her mother. She still visits every three weeks but now can spend her time in other ways.

Other Austin friends, Charlie and Ann arranged for a local restaurant to deliver a main meal at noon for his parents, who live in Kansas, when his eighty plus year-old mother injured her right hand. Meals on Wheels were tried but found wanting. The restaurant cooks just the kinds of meals Charlie's parents like so they had one, good nourishing meal each day. At this writing, mom is back cooking again, but I think that solution is one of the most creative I have yet to find.

Courtland's cousin, Betty Ann, prepares a complete meal two or three times a week to take to her father's house. Actually uncle Alex is still active and able to prepare a meal but Betty Ann is a gourmet cook plus she and her husband, Eddie, stay and eat the meal with uncle Alex and his older sister, aunt Mary. As Betty Ann says, "Aunt Mary would rather we come there than have her over here. This way we can dine together and daddy gets a break from cooking."

CLEANING CHORES

Heidi's mother is being cared for by her 80-year-old father. Heidi lives in northern Alabama and her parents live in Tennessee, too far away for her to personally provide regular help, but she supports her father's efforts by paying for a weekly cleaning lady. She encourages her father to take advantage of community offerings for respite care so he can get out occasionally. She assures him that taking good care of himself is the most important thing he can do for his wife.

Elderly people often lack the energy or the strength to clean their homes but they sometimes object to having a stranger clean their house, as well as being concerned about the cost involved. My brother and I arranged for a lady to clean mom's house while she was keeping vigil at the hospital with our ill stepfather. Felix's son, Max, was expected and we wanted the house nice and clean. WRONG MOVE. When mom came home, exhausted and grieving, and found a complete stranger "tearing up" her house, she unceremoniously threw her out. She later apologized but I know we had handled the matter badly. We learned our lesson. When she needed a gardener, Gene asked her if she would like to *interview* a willing candidate for the job. One problem we found with mom was her reluctance to pay the going rate for various jobs when she needed to hire someone. Our options were then twofold; we could talk her into paying by reminding her this was a cost for staying in her own home, or, the other option was to split the cost between the two of us and call it our "mother's day gift" or something like that.

PROVIDING PERSONAL ASSISTANCE

I have a cousin, Rita, who lives near her parents' home and goes daily to give her invalid mother a bath, make sure the bed is clean and comfortable and any other personal care which her elderly father can't provide. She cooks their main meal each day and does the heavier cleaning chores. Rita has done this for *nine years*! She says, "I couldn't have done this without the constant support I have received from my children and grandchildren." Her gift of love and service has allowed her parents to remain together in their own home instead of having to split them up by placing one in a nursing home.

Another cousin, Jan, has taken early retirement and moved close to her parents' home where she can go with her parents on doctors' visits, monitor medications and basically support them in all ways as their strength fails. Not only are Uncle Ray and Aunt Millie delighted to have her companionship, but additionally, they draw great reassurance from knowing she is close by if and when they need her.

GENERAL HELP

One service to provide is to look in the yellow pages and make a few calls exploring community services which the elderly person may access. Making the elderly person aware of resources they can tap into can be a great help. You may need to remind them they can order some foods delivered and use transportation services designed for elderly and handicapped persons. Senior citizens clubs are also a good resource for available services. If they, like my thrifty mom, protest about some costs which *you* feel are acceptable and well within their ability to pay, it may help to remind them that they are extending their stay in their own home and this **IS** the rainy day they have saved for.

LIVE-IN ASSISTANCE

Our friend, Eric, lives in Austin, Texas. His mother lives in a small town two-hundred and fifty miles north of Austin. As Eric's mother grew feeble, Eric was grateful that Mother Lloyd had a companion 20 years her junior who had lived with the family for years. Hilda had been a "displaced" person when Eric's parents had brought her to live with them in the 1940s. Hilda, in her early seventies, did the cooking, provided company for Eric's widowed mother and of course provided the surveillance we spoke of.

Then one of those little unexpected events we should all expect occurred. Hilda developed a debilitating disease which affected her mentally and physically. Not only was Eric now unable to depend on Hilda's help with Mother Lloyd, but since Hilda had no family, Eric needed to provide for her care.

With two ladies in the house who needed looking after, Eric looked into hiring some "round the clock" help for all the household and caregiving tasks. Letty Black, who had cleaned for Mother Lloyd for many years became his first and most reliable resource. She was willing to fill one shift and through her church resources found other ladies who were willing to fill other shifts, take weekend hours and be backup for ladies who were ill or needed time off.

Letty was paid an additional amount to "supervise" and make sure all shifts were covered. When Letty could no longer fill the position, Eric, for a time, found help through the local Elder Care agency.

At present, he staffs two 12 hour shifts. He has four people on payroll, covering for relief and days off. It is amazing that he is able to accomplish this. Finding good people who will remain on the job can be a real challenge. Eric says he has been successful because in this community there are many dependable Christian women who are retired and are willing to care for two elderly women at a price which is doable. I asked him if he is spending less per month by providing "in house" care for both ladies than he would spend if each lady were living in a nursing home. His reply was that considering the maintenance on the home, food and utility costs, it is costing more to keep the ladies at home. "This is not an economy decision," was his answer.

I don't wish to leave the impression that this solution leaves Eric with no responsibilities. He makes the long drive north about every third weekend and keeps in touch by phone the rest of the time.

Additionally, I should remind you that, payrolls mean accurate record keeping, withholding taxes, depositing taxes and filing quarterly federal payroll tax forms and if applicable, state quarterly payroll tax forms. At the end of each calendar year, there are W-2's to send and more forms to file. Also, one might consider carrying a Workers' Compensation policy, even if your state doesn't require you to do so. Remember we are living in a time when injured people sue and are often awarded large settlements if they are injured on the job. And even if you are never sued, you would certainly wish to provide for someone who was injured while caring for your parent.

This solution would not work for all families. The cost may be impossible for some. The staffing could be a nightmare. However, this creative solution is working for Eric and is a story I wanted to share with you.

SHARED HOUSING

If your parent's problem is loneliness and fear of staying alone, one solution may be **shared housing.** In a community where rents are high or there are many college students, it may be possible to find a satisfactory person to share the parent's home. This only works, of course, when the parent is able to look after him/herself. There may be a Shared Housing Council in your community. One in California had social events where people who had already been screened for likes and dislikes could meet and decide if they might try living together.

My mother shortcut this process by simply running an advertisement in the newspaper for a "working man, non-smoking" to share her house. My brother almost had apoplexy when he found out what she had done. He had a mental picture of a rapist or murderer answering her advertisement. However, thanks to whatever guardian angel watches over little old ladies, both young men whom she found this way were fine. One was wonderful beyond our wildest dreams. He did errands, helped out around the house and even found a couple of television shows which they both enjoyed and regularly watched them with her. This provided her with much needed companionship and a sense of security. This extended the length of time she was able to remain in her own home.

The October 1995 issue of AARP BULLETIN carried an article on shared housing or (their name) "joint living." The article states that one in eight Americans age 45 and older lives with extended family, roommates, partners, grandchildren, boarders or caregivers.

The article goes on to describe the experience three siblings have in sharing a home. They pool their money and share almost all activities together. It seems they have many common interests, get along well and are meeting each other's need for companionship as well as stretching their retirement dollars. They were living in the town where they had grown up so no one had to be "uprooted."

A grandchild can be a good companion for an elderly person. We knew of one family who had a difficult teenager. When the teenager went to live with the grandmother, the family was afraid she would continue her rebellious ways and make her grandmother's life miserable. Instead, she voluntarily kept rules that she resented in her parents' home. She helped out around the house and generally behaved in a responsible way, much to the relief and amazement of her bedraggled parents.

For the parent who is still mentally competent and physically able to care for their personal needs, shared housing can be a great solution to loneliness and fear of being in a house alone.

SUMMARY

With some commitment from family and friends, as well as some creative thinking, it may be possible to extend a parent's time in his or her own home. The things which need to be provided for as the parents grow less able to do for themselves are surveillance, nourishing meals, cleaning and household chores, general help with transportation and shopping. If the parent gets unable to attend to personal care, outside assistance can be an option. Even so, maintaining a parent's own home sometimes is not the best choice. In the next chapter we will look at residences which provide additional living options for the elderly.

5 | Other Living Options

"My parents didn't want to move to Florida,
but they turned sixty, and it was the law."
Jerry Seinfeld

Since there are times when it may be best for an elderly parent to move from home, this chapter will list various types of retirement options which are offered commercially. We will discuss some of the advantages of each choice as well as some of the disadvantages of each.

CONTINUING-CARE RETIREMENT COMMUNITIES

Continuing-care retirement communities are an interesting option for those individuals or couples who wish to make long range plans while they are still active. "It's a place where they can grow old with the comfort of knowing that their long-term-care needs will be met," says an article in the June 1996 issue of *Kiplinger's Personal Finance Magazine*. This article goes on to list ten top-rated communities in several states.

My first reaction to the article is that these communities seem perfect for some retired people. One thing I like is the idea that if one spouse needs nursing care, that is provided on the same campus so they need not be separated.

The next reaction I had is that unless one of these communities is close to where the elderly person already lives, moving to one might mean leaving family, friends and church. One would again ask, what one would give up and what would one gain if that were the case.

My neighbor, Mrs. Ward, is considering moving to a continuing-care community because she fears that if she ever has to live in a nursing home her funds would be eaten up leaving her penniless and nothing for her heirs. In Austin, I spoke to Mary Dunneback who works for Life Care Communities. They administer a lot of these types of communities. The one in Austin for which Mary does the marketing will guarantee that the entire estate will **not** be eaten up in nursing costs.

If you, like Mrs. Ward, are considering a continuing-care community because you fear your funds will be eaten up in nursing care, it is important to know that nursing care may never be necessary. The *Kiplinger's RETIREMENT REPORT*, December 1995 states that "A 65-year old's chances of being in a (nursing) home at some point range from about 20% to 50% depending on the study. That sounds worse than it is because studies often include short-term nursing-home stays that occur after hospitalization."

Four things to consider. (1) Does a continuing-care community make sense financially? (2) Are the current residents a good match for the person considering moving there? In other words do they have similar interests and backgrounds? (3) Will this move take one away from family, friends and church? (4) What assurance do you have that the nursing care will be the quality you want if or when you need it?

INDEPENDENT LIVING FACILITIES

These are the common man's Waldorf Astoria. For the three years my father lived in one of these facilities, and the seven years my mother lived in them, we had very positive experiences! We were living in southern California which was one of the first areas to offer this living option, and there were many to choose from. The first one I chose for my dad was not right for him (it was a little too hoity-toity), but we were able to find one that was right for a simple country lad.

If you are fortunate enough to have several in your area, they may look something like this: There is a room or an apartment for a month by month rental fee which can be surprisingly reasonable. (We found that a kitchen is totally unnecessary. The most a parent may want is to be able to keep a few sodas and this can be done by providing them with an "office" refrigerator.) Three meals a day are provided in a common dining room. There are many common rooms such as television rooms, game rooms, a library, and large rooms where residents can gather for entertainment, book reviews, a special movie or just a place for them to entertain several guests. Snacks are usually available. Residents can have guests for a meal. Sometimes a small charge is made for guest meals. Other places allow for a certain number of guest meals per month.

There is someone on duty twenty-four hours a day. The residents' rooms are equipped with (usually two) emergency cords, one in the bathroom, one in an area where they may want to place their bed, so help can be summoned from their bed if they become ill in the night.

Many have patios and gardens. The first one my mother lived in even had garden boxes available for those residents who wanted to plant flowers. That one allowed some small pets! Some have classes, craft programs and special outings.

Transportation was provided in all the retirement homes in which my parents resided. There were regular days for banking, visits to a shopping mall, and if the resident's church was close enough, they would provide transportation there. My son-in-law's mother lives in a residence which provides limousine service! Three trips a month are free, after the third trip, a fee of five dollars is charged. Of course this is in Newport Beach, California, wouldn't ya' know!

Residents' rooms are cleaned daily. Most provide linens. Some provide furniture although the residents are encouraged to bring their own furniture so they have their own things around them. Upon request, the staff will dispense any medications the residents are taking. And if a resident doesn't show up at meal time, a member of the staff will check to make sure they are all right.

They don't provide any nursing care. If the resident is ill they usually will bring a tray at meal times for three or four days. After that, the resident must make other arrangements. Once when my mother was ill, not wishing to uproot her from her home, we hired a nurse to care for her until she was well.

41

Other Living Options

But we could have brought her home with us for a few days.

Different facilities attract and cater to different kinds of residents. Some we looked at were very picky that all residents were mentally clear, and physically able to take care of themselves. They often presented a glamorous image; crystal chandeliers, fresh flowers and linens on the dining tables, etc.

Other facilities were more for people who weren't looking for so much glamour. We found that each facility took on a different personality. The people who lived there could be as varied as the ambience of the facility. That was why we liked the month to month rent. It was important to find a good match for the parent.

ASSISTED LIVING

As mother grew less able to attend to her personal care, Assisted Living facilities were being developed in our area. At first she was able to live in Independent Living Residences which provided "just a little more" in the way of assistance. We paid a bit extra and someone would help with her bath and dressing. Finally she could no longer undress herself at night. She could not even put toothpaste on her toothbrush. She needed the higher level of care provided in an assisted living facility. The monthly rent was higher, of course, and we were surprised to learn how much more some charged than others. You will need to check out what is offered in the more expensive facilities to see if the additional expense is worthwhile.

The resident still has his/her own room, but the staffing has been increased so there are people who can assist the elderly resident with their personal care. This can mean help with baths, dressing and assisting them to the dining room. Facilities like this usually will take a resident who has some dementia. They may not, however, take a resident who may wander off. It depends on how well they are set up for security. We found, too, that some would not take a nonambulatory resident. In California there are laws regulating staff per resident ratios depending on whether the residents can exit the building unassisted should an emergency such as a fire arise. For that reason, some refused nonambulatory residents to keep staffing costs down.

I believe that many people living in nursing homes could be living in Assisted Living facilities which, I think, have many advantages over nursing homes. The most important advantage is the continued sense of independence and privacy. Additionally the cost is much less, and the general atmosphere of more active, healthier people can make living in an assisted living residence much pleasanter.

PERSONAL CARE

I am not sure what these facilities are called in various parts of the country. I will define them as residences for elderly people who need personal care, and which are small — usually in private homes converted for such purposes. They are often staffed by the owner with some additional help. They take just a few residents. When we moved to Austin, Texas, we discovered that the Assisted Living facilities as we had known them in California didn't exist. However, we found several good Personal Care facilities.

They are not always easy to find. Many in Austin are not licensed so aren't found in the yellow pages. You have to get on the jungle drums. Once you find one, they usually know where the others are. So if one is full or too far away, they will usually tell you about the others.

If you consider a facility which isn't licensed, remember that what the state licensing agency would have done, you must do. It is up to you to review safety procedures such as smoke detectors. Make sure the pantry is well stocked. You need to show up at mealtimes often enough to determine that the residents are well fed. You may be surprised to learn that providing good quality meals is so costly in terms of preparation hours and food costs, that this is an area that is sometimes short-changed. You need to make sure that not only are good meals provided but that the foods meet your parents' preference and health needs.

One challenge, we found, was that in most of the houses, the bathroom doors had not been modified to accommodate a walker or wheelchair. This eliminated several personal care homes which might otherwise have been suitable for mom.

You will need to ask staffing questions. Who is on staff when the primary caregiver is out? Does the primary caregiver have days off? (If days off are not provided, the caregiver may "burn-out" and your parent may not receive the level of care they need, or there may be a series of new people all the time.) Ask about the number of people on staff? How long have they been with the facility? If there are frequent turnovers with the staff, your parent must constantly adjust to new people. Also, the people you interviewed and thought would give your parent good care may leave, and the new staff may not be suitable. We had some real horror stories when staffing changed.

One thing I observed was, did the person showing us around talk to mother, or ignore her and talk only to me. Also, when they were showing a room, did they knock before entering it or just barge right in showing no respect for the privacy of the resident? What is their attitude toward the current residents? These things are clues as to how they view the residents and the kind of respect which will be shown to your parent.

Once my mother became an almost total invalid, even losing her ability to speak, I found that it was vital that I monitor carefully the kind of care she was receiving and who was providing it.

The advantage I found in using a personal care home rather than a nursing home, was the "personal care." Being small, they provided some personalized care that the nursing home could not. Two disadvantages were that there were fewer recreational activities offered and the quality of care was not as consistent.

I will discuss when and how to choose a nursing home in the next chapter.

FINDING RETIREMENT FACILITIES

THE DIRECTORY OF RETIREMENT FACILITIES, published annually by Health Care Information Analysts, Inc. (800-568-3282), lists more than 22,000 facilities nationwide, including retirement communities and nursing homes. The entries list basic contact information, types of living arrangements offered, entry and monthly fees, the number of units and residents, whether the facility is for-profit or not-for-profit and more. Because the directory is nearly 1,400 pages, it costs $249. However, it's available in many libraries.

Local Area Agencies on Aging (AAA) can also help you find out what's available in your city or state. They can often provide lists of local retirement communities and assisted living facilities, or refer you to other resources.

To locate the AAA for your community, check the blue government pages in your phone book or look in the yellow pages under "Aging" or "Senior Citizens." Or call the number for Eldercare Locator (800-677-1116), a public service funded by the United States Administration on Aging.

If you are considering a buy-in, move-to retirement community you might consider two books: *The 50 Best Retirement Communities in America* ($14.95; St. Martin's Press, 175 Fifth Avenue, New York, NY 10010; 800-288-2131) by Alice and Fred Lee; and *The Only Retirement Guide You'll Ever Need,* ($14.95; Poseidon Press) by Kathryn and Ross Petras. Like the advertisement for Yellow Pages said, "Let your fingers do the walking." Your yellow pages may be a good resource. Decide what answers you want. If the person you talk to cannot answer your questions, ask them who might be able to provide you with answers. I always used a large note pad, made good notes and wrote down the name of the person I talked to so that as I had other questions, I could ask for the same person.

FLEXIBILITY

I want to emphasize again that there are lots of surprises. The more flexible your plans are, the less chance you will get locked in to something where the parent is unhappy. That is why I believe one shouldn't sell the parent's home right away. It gives a parent comfort to know that they can go home. This may give a parent the confidence to try an alternative living arrangement. Additionally, if they find they just can't adjust, perhaps going home can be given another try. They may be more willing to have help at home which they refused before, in order to get another chance to be at home. Shirley and I have wondered if Howard would have been willing to have a health care worker in on a regular basis as a trade for being able to go home.

Remember, you need to think of living solutions in terms of months, not years. My goal was to keep my mother from having to move into a nursing home. I evaluated every living arrangement which lasted even a short time, on that basis. Some of the places we moved mother changed after she moved there. Some of the places were not as represented. Sometimes we had to move her because her needs had changed. One hot, humid summer, I moved mom three times. The best advice I can offer is to know where you can locate a pickup truck and someone with a strong back whom you can call to help you.

6 | Nursing Homes

"Be nice to your children, for they will choose your rest home."
Phyllis Diller

I will begin this chapter with an apology to all good nursing home administrators who find my attitude toward nursing homes too negative. I know there are good nursing home administrators. I also believe that you have one of the most challenging jobs anyone can have. Your facility must meet the needs of people who are ill, sometimes mentally demented, often unhappy . . . and that just covers the family members of your residents.

I believe that running a nursing home *well* is about as challenging as running General Motors. And I have yet to meet a nursing home administrator who receives a salary nearly as high as the CEO of General Motors.

Mary McMahon, a nursing home administrator whom I asked to review this chapter, has asked me to tone down some of the negativity, and I have attempted to do so. She points out that many of the residents who come to live in the nursing home she administers are very relieved to be free of the worry and work of being alone. Additionally, they enjoy the social interaction with other residents and the many activities the facility provides.

I have placed this chapter after the other alternatives which I suggest as living options for elderly people, however, because that is just how I continue to view the nursing home option. I consider a nursing home to be an option only when other options have been considered and found not adequate. I certainly don't want to put a burden of guilt on those of you who decided that a nursing home is the best, perhaps only, option for your loved one.

NURSING HOME FUNCTIONS

There are many different kinds of nursing homes. Some are geared to provide acute level nursing care. They can provide the kind of care which enables a patient to leave a costly hospital bed for a less costly nursing home bed. Other nursing homes function much on the level of the Assisted Living Facilities described in chapter five. These latter are often found in more rural communities which have no Assisted Living Facilities.

Let me describe to you the one which Mary McMahon administers. It is located in the "hill country" about 20 miles west of Austin. Hill Country Care is in the small country town of Dripping Springs. The citizens of the community decided to provide a nonprofit nursing facility for their elderly. Additionally, adjacent to the nursing home, are cottages for independent living residents who can avail themselves of meals in the dining room and participate in the recreational activities offered.

Ms. McMahon has been able to staff with people from the community who are caring and reliable. I don't know if this is characteristic of country towns, but I suspect it is. One benefit is that there is very little staff turnover. The people on staff are accountable to each other. After all they are neighbors. The staff seems to really care about their elderly residents, many of whom are also neighbors. The fee to stay there is reasonable and since it is a nonprofit organization, all the fees are returned to the facility for staffing and perks for the residents. As Ms. McMahon says, "Since we are nonprofit, any funds we receive above our operating costs, can be spent on things which make this a better facility."

There are many community volunteers, including local schoolchildren who "adopt" a grandparent. It is probably a model facility of its kind. It has only one major drawback that I can see — the bathrooms aren't large enough for use by a person with a walker or wheelchair. If you live in a rural area without some of the different levels of residential options I have described, I hope you have something like Hill Country Care.

CHOOSING A NURSING HOME

Choosing a nursing home is about like choosing a mate for life. It is important to get it right and you need to know what you are looking for. One of the things which may make your choice so critical, is that you may be placing a parent who is unable to discern good care from bad care. They may be unable to communicate with you just what goes on when you aren't there. And, they may not even be able to communicate with the staff.

My first experience with placing any of my family in a nursing home was when my father broke a hip while living in an independent care facility. His hip required surgery to mend the break and the doctors told us to take him to nursing home "X" because they had an excellent physical therapy department where daddy could be trained to walk again.

You need to know that the shock of his injury plus the anesthetic and surgery knocked out most of what was left of my father's mind. There was no way he was going to be retrained to walk! That would have taken strength of will in addition to hours of effort. Daddy only knew he wanted to be comfortable. But the nursing home was unable to provide even safety and comfort. On the third or fourth day after his hip surgery, daddy received his first therapy session. When I walked into his room for a visit, he was sitting in a wheelchair. He was totally motionless and an ashen gray color. I thought at first he was dead, then I saw the beads of sweat on his forehead. And, I also saw that his hands were bloodless from gripping the arm rest of the wheelchair as he attempted to hold his weight up off his painful, injured hip.

It seemed it took forever for me to find someone to help me get him into bed. As near as I could piece events together, daddy had been rolled up from therapy and *left*! I had no idea how long he had sat there on that injured hip. He couldn't tell me and none of the staff had the time or inclination to enlighten me.

I could tell you more horror stories.. . . about how the staff didn't measure his urine and I found him with his bladder about to burst, or how I found him tied in his bed when he got stronger. By this time we had a family team to (as our daughter, Cindy, put it) "hit this place four and five times a day." On one of my early morning "inspection trips" the director told me that I could no longer visit so early. She explained that early morning hours were bath and breakfast times and please not to come anymore before eleven o'clock. *I explained to her that her facility had almost killed my father, and I would come any time day or night that I wished to.* Those may not have been my exact words.

That was the only time in my life I ever threatened to sue anyone.

By the mercy of God we all finally realized that daddy was not ever going to benefit from the physical therapy. We found a really good nursing home and moved him there. I cannot describe the contrast between the two. He lived there eleven days and then he had a stroke which killed him. I am so thankful to God and to that wonderful nursing staff that he was in such a safe and comfortable place his last days.

From dad's last experience, I know that there are good nursing homes. If you can plan ahead before placing a parent, visit several times. Visit different hours during the day, including evening hours. Talk to the staff. Talk to patients. Talk to family members of the patients. Observe how responsive the staff is to a bell. Check out the meals. Observe how much time is given to those patients who cannot feed themselves. Look for outside areas which patients can use. Are there pets, plants and recreational activities? What is the staff turnover? How does the facility smell? Either urine or cover-up scents may alert you to slack cleaning procedures or residents who are left in wet diapers. Are patients who are demented and may cause distress to other patients by constantly calling out or being belligerent somewhat segregated? Are there activities which provide mental stimulation? Are there regular exercise programs commensurate with the residents' physical strength and skills? Are there calendars and seasonal decorations which help the residents keep track of what time of year it is? Watch how the staff interacts with the residents. Do they speak to and touch the patients as they pass by? Do they seem hurried and overworked?

Rosalynn Carter has written a wonderful book, *Helping Yourself Help Others* (Times Books, a division of Random House, Inc., 1994). It is an excellent book, full of helpful resource material. I recommend her book for many reasons other than what she has to say about choosing a nursing home. But I think this is a good place to mention her book.

Also, in August 1995, *Consumer Reports* began a three-part series discussing nursing homes. In September, the article dealt with who pays for nursing homes. They discussed what could be expected from Medicare and Medicaid. The October issue talked of assisted living and home care. Your local library should have these issues. I would suggest that you read all three articles.

WHEN SHOULD YOU PLACE A PARENT IN A NURSING HOME?

This is my personal opinion, but I think you place a parent in a nursing home when there is no other acceptable option. I believe that a nursing home is for people who need nursing care. There may be no good "Personal Care" or "Board and Care" places in your community. Or you may find a nursing home which provides excellent care as well as recreational opportunities so you feel confident it is a good place for your parent.

When an elderly person has little or no mind left they may be indifferent to where they are. (However, even people with advanced dementia, can often sense how their caregivers feel about them.) Other times a person with dementia may become so belligerent that no family member or smaller Board and Care facility can cope with them.

BALANCE

Although I consider a nursing home a last resort, I am well aware that they can be an only option in some cases. I have a mother-in-law in a nursing home. Even though it is a good one, she is not happy. However, she was no less unhappy in her daughter's home. Her mind is failing; she, too, has broken a hip and needs a high level of physical care. We all agree that placing her in a nursing home is the best choice.

To be fair with nursing home staffs, most of them are kind and do the best job they can. Usually the pay is low and the work hard. Old people are not always nice to be with and they are not always easy to love. If you have a parent in a nursing home where you are concerned about their care, and if you and they are able, bring them home for a day or two. There is no better way of learning just what your parent needs or discovering undetected problems. . . . and, there is no better way of learning to appreciate the staff of the nursing home.

DON'T LEAVE THEM THERE TO ROT

Parents who know where and who they are and are physically able to be taken out occasionally **should be!** Many patients in nursing homes can be taken out by the family. They can go for drives and to restaurants. They can join their family for holiday meals. They can even be kept overnight. There is no need to be intimidated by wheelchairs or diapers. A little resolve is all that is needed. And a willingness to be embarrassed sometimes.

When my father was still living in nursing home X, I found him in such a rage at being tied to his bed, that (after threatening the staff with unnamed horrors if I ever found him tied again, and inquiring if they received their training at Dachau) I helped him dress, put him in a wheelchair and we went for a walk. A short way from the nursing home was a Coco's restaurant, so we decided to go in for a cup of coffee. We spent a pleasant few minutes drinking coffee and watching the tropical fish in the restaurant's large fish tank. Then daddy said he had to use the rest room. What to do? I put him back in his wheelchair and wheeled him to the men's room door. After knocking and calling loudly, I opened the door and we went in. I wheeled him to the urinal, got behind him and helped him to his feet. With me supporting him from behind he was able to keep his weight on his uninjured hip. Even though daddy was a heavy man and I am just slightly over five feet, supporting him wasn't very difficult. I was feeling rather smug about how well I was managing when it began to nag at me how . . long . . . this . . was . . . taking. It was then that I learned that ill, elderly gentlemen don't just **do it**; it sometimes takes a while. I thought of running water to help things along, but I couldn't reach the faucet without letting go of daddy. I am prone to fantasize at times when I am trapped in an awkward situation (yes, there have been other moments in my life which were awkward). In my mind, I could see the headlines in the local paper, "Middle-aged mother of three arrested for molesting elderly gentleman in Coco's rest room."

As I say, take your elderly parent out of the nursing home for pleasant little outings. A little resolve is all that is needed.

SUMMARY

For many families, a nursing home is the best, perhaps the only realistic choice available for an elderly parent. Even so, many children, especially daughters, experience deep feelings of guilt. There are support groups available to help you. Remember that we aren't responsible for their growing old and sick, and it is not always possible to provide exactly the kind of care for them which we wish. Often the best we can do is choose carefully, monitor their care, and if they are mentally and physically able, take them out often.

7 | Living with the "Kids"

"Aunt Alma," I asked yesterday,
"Why you sticking Sitty in the 'tomb'?"
She got angry, "It ain't the 'tomb.'
It's The Asylum For The Aged."
"Then why you sticking Sitty in The Asylum For The Aged?"
"Victoria, I'm over eighty. I can't care for her no more."
From *When I Am an Old Woman I Shall Wear Purple*

Is it a good decision for an elderly parent to move in with one of their children? The object of this chapter is to help you determine the impact on the life of the adult child and their family as well as the impact on the elderly parent when the decision is made to have mom or dad move in with one of their children.

Even with many other options available, it is still quite common for an elderly parent to live with a child. Many times this decision is made because both parent and child feel that this is the way things are *supposed* to be done. There are times when this is a good decision for the parent as well as the caregiver. Sometimes it is not. And sometimes there *are* almost no other choices.

I believe that a child should not feel guilty for not bringing a parent to live with them. If caring for the parent is a crushing burden to the caregiver or their family, everyone suffers, the parent as well as the caregiver. I don't believe that caring for a parent at home is a measure of one's love. When we placed my mother-in-law in a lovely retirement home, she said we were putting her in an "old folks home" because we didn't love her. That was her dementia talking. We did and do love her. We knew that the retirement hotel would provide her with all she needed in terms of safety, good food, recreation and other elderly people for companionship. We also knew that in our home (where she thought she should be living) she would be alone all day while we were at work with no stimulation and activities to keep her busy.

Even though many years ago it was taken for granted that an elderly person, when he/she could no longer live alone would move in with a child, if some of the stories passed down are to be believed, these were not always happy situations. My neighbor, Edna, told me that her mother said, "When we get too old to live alone, if we still have our minds, we will go live in a home. If we don't have enough mind left to realize we can no longer live alone, you put us in one. Don't take us to live with you. Years ago your grandparents came to live with us and it ruined our lives. We don't want to ruin your life that way."

We need to remember that many years ago when an elderly parent moved in with one of their children, the parent might have been only in their seventies and the child in their forties or fifties. Now, with people living longer, elderly parents are being cared for by elderly children. In one case we know of, the mother is almost 100 years old and the daughter almost 80 years old.

HOW WELL WILL IT WORK?

In determining why sometimes caring for a parent at home is a successful effort and why sometimes it is not, we will look at several factors:

(1) The personalities/temperament of the people involved
(2) The amount and kind of care the parent requires
(3) Amount of support the caregiver will have
(4) Opportunities for the caregiver to go have fun and recreation
(5) The house size and layout
(6) The physical and mental condition of the caregiver
(7) Other demands on the caregiver's time and energy
(8) Recreational opportunities for the elderly person
(9) Does the elderly person have dementia?

I will tell you some true stories as clearly as I can so you can put yourself into the picture and see how you and your family might fare.

ELLIS/LAWSON FAMILIES

Birdie and Leroy Ellis live in Southern California. They have a large house. When mom and dad grew older, they bought the house next door and moved mom and dad there so they could provide surveillance and support. When dad died, mom was failing mentally and physically to the extent that the Ellises moved mom into their home. She had her own wing of the house complete with two bedrooms and bathroom. Then Mother Ellis' daughter, Lynn and her husband, Tom bought the house next door. Birdie and Leroy both had full-time jobs, but Lynn was a stay-at-home mom of two teenagers.

During the day Lynn would go next door and supervise mom's bath and fix her breakfast and lunch. Evenings, mom dined with Leroy and Birdie or in her room. One of them helped her get ready for bed before retiring to their own room upstairs. The last few months of Mother Ellis' life, Leroy or Birdie took turns sleeping downstairs in the adjoining bedroom to be nearby in case they were needed.

Mother Ellis spent her days watching television and dozing in her chair until one day her heart stopped and she went to be with her husband.

We all watched this family with admiration and a little envy. They seemed to have all the pieces in place. What made this such a success story?

The arrangement with the two families sharing the responsibility for Mother Ellis split the physical and mental demands in half. Both families pulled their load and helped out where needed so that each family had some time off from caregiving responsibilities. Neither family kept a "score book" on what the other family was contributing.

Mother Ellis was comparatively easy to care for. She was able to be left alone for short periods because she could use the bathroom herself, she didn't wander off, and she felt no need to be in the kitchen around the stove. She required little in the way of entertainment. She was not a complaining lady, nor was she demanding. Leroy and Birdie had their own space and privacy.

Additionally, the Ellises and Lynn Lawson were healthy, high energy people. Even though Tom had some health problems which prevented him from helping with Mother Ellis, the two teenage children were willing and dependable helpers. All the family members were busy people but they were busy with interesting things which energized them. And each had enough free time to go on with their lives.

RITA'S STORY (NOT TO BE CONFUSED WITH "COUSIN RITA")

My friend Rita took care of her invalid mother many years before I knew her. Here is her story as she told it to me.

Rita, her husband, John and their two young teenagers were living in Corpus Christi, Texas, when Rita and her sister, Jean, determined that Mother Walker needed nursing care. Both sisters agreed that they preferred caring for their mother at home rather than placing her in a nursing home. Jean was a schoolteacher and also had a husband who was in poor health so Rita offered to be the primary caregiver with Jean providing support.

Mother Walker was moved into Rita's home. Her mind was unimpaired as was her keen since of humor. She was a total invalid, however, needing help in getting up, bathing, dressing, going to the bathroom, etc. Rita's whole family took an interest in Mother Walker. John is a generous man in every sense of the word. He is generous with things, time and help. Additionally he can capably take over any household duty from shopping and cooking to cleaning. Naturally the teenagers were involved in their own teenage things, but they too were willing helpers and Rita would pay them for extras. Taking full responsibility for Mother Walker for an evening was labeled an "extra." Staying with her while Rita made a quick trip to the market was not.

John says that whenever he came home very late from work he would look in on Mother Walker. Often he would find her still awake, and he would stop and talk with her for awhile. He has fond memories of those visits.

As Rita looks back on those years she says that caring for her mother in her home was not *easy*, but it was *not a crushing burden*, and she is very glad she was able to do it.

There are several factors which made this effort a success. First was the support which Rita received from several sources. Rita's sister was a support, even though she couldn't carry half the load of caregiving, she was an emotional support and additionally she was a backup for physical care during family vacations.

Rita's family seemed ideally suited to having Mother Walker in their home. Their willingness to contribute something to her care and enjoy her company made a huge difference to Rita and provided needed mental stimulation and entertainment for Mother Walker. Rita says her family's help was the single most important factor in making the time she cared for her mother successful.

Another very important factor was the relief which Rita was able to have from a local Nurses Registry. Rita committed two days a week for her own activities. Someone from the Nurses Registry would come and relieve Rita for the entire day. This break rested Rita and allowed her to see friends and pursue hobbies. The Registry was also used on Sunday Mornings so the family could attend church services and go out to lunch.

Mother Walker's good sense of humor and her noncomplaining attitude made her presence in the home pleasant. Additionally each family member had their own space and privacy.

I believe that one of the most important factors in this success story is Rita's temperament. She is an extremely balanced person. She knew how to make sensible decisions about what was important and how to "pace" herself so that she didn't burn out. She determined just what level of care would be necessary for her mother's comfort and well being; beyond that, she did not go. As an example, she decided that her mother didn't need to be bathed and dressed every day in order to be healthy and happy. Thus she was freed from a tiring and time consuming task which she delegated to the nurses who came to help.

She was *reasonable* about the amount of time and energy she gave to her mother. Both women benefited from this balance. Because Rita was able to pursue her own interests she was a happier and more energetic caregiver. Because Rita was reasonable about the amount of help she could expect from her children, they did not resent helping. Rita did not consider herself "super woman." And since other members of the family provided Mother Walker with company, her mother's entertainment didn't fall entirely to Rita.

THELMA AND HER MOTHER-IN-LAW

Virginia Blake, an acquaintance here in Austin, told me this story about her friend Thelma who lives in Chapel Hill, North Carolina. Thelma and George became concerned with his mother living alone in her big house in Milwaukee. Mother Bergstrom lived a very isolated life. If she had ever had many friends, they were gone now. The concern was that she would fall ill with no neighbors, family, friends, church or community support to provide her necessary care. Mother Bergstrom, at ninety years of age, was still strong, but her isolation and the realization that her health could not continue indefinitely made George and Thelma wish she would move close to them.

Virginia and Thelma's other friends encouraged her to find a retirement hotel for her mother-in-law because Thelma's health was not good. Thelma, whose sons were grown, pointed out that there was plenty of room for Mother Bergstrom to live with her and George. Thelma is a mother-hen type. She is a loving, giving person who wants to make everyone's life good. She is a "fixer." I have come to the conclusion that "fixers" are the first to burn out as caregivers. "Fixers" can't leave anything alone which they believe can be improved even slightly. It is difficult for them to accept less than perfect conditions. Believing she could manage the extra work, Thelma invited Mother Bergstrom to move into their home.

The Battle Begins. George and Mother Bergstrom had never gotten on. Each evening, when George came home from work, those two hardheaded people picked up the disagreements which they had never resolved. Thelma was appalled. She was from a loving family where quarrels were rare. She couldn't believe George would speak to his mother in such a way. She pleaded with George to be kind and not quarrel with his mother. His response was, "She starts it." Which Thelma had to acknowledge was usually true. Neither mother or son would cut the other any slack.

Depression. Mother Bergstrom was deeply depressed. She didn't want to live and had no faith in God or a better life beyond this one. She was estranged from her daughter, couldn't get along with her son, and had no hobbies or interests. In short, she had none of the things which make life worthwhile. Thelma began talking to Mother Bergstrom about the love of God and the healing and forgiveness He offers. She tried to provide Mother Bergstrom with things which might interest her, good books, good music, visits from her grandchildren. Friends watched as Thelma expended enormous energy and emotions on this lady. They worried about Thelma and her own health.

Declining Health. As expected, Mother Bergstrom's health began to decline. So did Thelma's. Mother B. was less and less able to care for her personal needs. In spite of her own declining health, Thelma increased her effort to meet Mother B's needs. Thelma bathed her, helped her dress, fixed her hair. Mother Bergstrom didn't have much appetite. Thelma worked harder preparing tasty meals which would tempt Mother B's appetite. Thelma fretted that Mother B. didn't drink enough water, didn't get enough exercise, wouldn't leave the house. Friends wondered who would go first, Thelma or Mother B.

Other Demands. Thelma had no help with the housework, shopping or meal preparation. She had ministries at church which she continued to meet faithfully. George contributed little around the house but continued to expect the same level of comfort and attention from Thelma to which he had become accustomed. The college age sons were in and out of the home for various lengths of time with dirty laundry and their college friends. Thelma, without the balance which Rita possessed, gave to everyone . . . tried to do it all. But no one, including Thelma, took care of Thelma.

Analysis. Thelma took on a difficult, demanding task which she wasn't physically strong enough to do. The conflict between her husband and mother-in-law created great stress for her. Mother Bergstrom's depression was difficult for a "fixer" to deal with. With her personality she took on all Mother B.'s problems, tried to fix them and then was stressed when she couldn't.

Conclusion. Finally, Thelma and George showed Mother B. some of the fine assisted living residences which their area offered. Mother B. found one she liked. Surprisingly, she adjusted very well. Or perhaps the family should not have been surprised. Mother B. had been used to a great deal of solitude and independence. Virginia didn't say, but my guess is that Mother B. was relieved to be away from Thelma's mother-hen personality and on her own again with only the impersonal assistance which the staff provided.

There were several tangible benefits from the move to the assisted living residence. She began to show real gratitude to Thelma for the loving care which she continued to provide. With his mother out of his home, George found less reason and opportunity to quarrel with her, and his visits with her were conflict free. Additionally, at the age of 95, Mother B. gave her life in faith to her Lord and was baptized. At her death, a year later, Thelma's health was stable and the family was finally at peace.

MY STORY

I, like Thelma am a "fixer." When I say "fixers" are not good personalities for caregivers, I speak from experience. We fixers believe we must fix every problem for all members of our family . . . occasionally our neighbors and the entire world. I believe I finally have insight to the source of my "fixer-ness." I believe that everything *can* and *should* be fixed. If God doesn't fix my world as quickly and in just the way I think it should be fixed, I step in and try to do it myself. I have repented of this sin, and am trying to allow God to transform me into a more accepting, trusting person .

I know now that I should have never tried to care for my mother in my home. She required a high level of care. She couldn't safely be left alone because her balance was so poor she would fall and even though only once injured herself, she couldn't get up. She had to have special foods, and her drooling made keeping her clean and dry a constant challenge. Wherever she went, I had to clean moisture off the floor so she or others wouldn't slip and fall.

I had too many other demands on my time and energy and little support. My daughter, Cindy, who lived next door and might have in other circumstances provided support, was caring for her new baby, Megan. She had just gone through a divorce and was wrapped in her own private sadness. *She* needed *my* support and help with her lively son, Nathan.

My husband didn't quarrel with mother, but he is not a mellow person and many things about having her in our house caused him distress. Naturally, with my personality, I assumed responsibility for his distress. I don't want to leave the impression that he was not supportive; he was. Or that he complained; he didn't. But I knew when he was uncomfortable with something and that was an added burden to me.

Mom was uncomplaining and had no dementia, but providing her with entertainment was a challenge because she had lost her ability to read and couldn't manage the remote controls on her television. She had lost, too, her ability to speak beyond an occasional word, so we couldn't have conversations which I, too, would have enjoyed.

Perhaps the biggest problem I had while I cared for mom was not having any opportunities for fun and recreation. We had just moved to Texas and established a family compound so we could share in the care of our grandchildren and try to diminish the damage divorce inflicts on children. When I wasn't taking care of mom, I was helping with Nathan and Megan. I couldn't have planned a better scenario for failure.

Leaving the town where I had grown up and lived for fifty years, robbed me of my friends and activities which I had learned to depend on for fun and relaxation. When I realized I needed to take a morning away from home, I had no place to go. I had no friends I could visit. I was living in the country far from anything I might want to do. Even attending church services or ladies Bible class required a major effort and a large block of time. Let me put you into the picture.

The church we had selected was a 45-minute drive from our house. At the time this decision was made, we didn't think this would be much of a problem. We did not realize that the children were not easily transportable. One hears stories of children who can be taken anywhere, even to Europe. Not the Vansickel children. Any trip longer than five miles with Megan and Nathan was a challenge equal to Magellan's trip around the Cape of Good Hope.

First we packed the car with toys, books, changes of clothes and food for the trip. Then the two Vansickel kids would be buckled protesting into car seats. Only the biggest, strongest and oldest of the adults got the favored job of driving. The other two (mom and grandma) were assigned the task of caring for two lively children for the next forty-five minutes. By the time we got to church, I didn't like anyone in the car except the children. The return trip home was the same story, except on the way home the children weren't so lively . . . they were tired and hungry. Occasionally we made the mistake of stopping at a restaurant. Texans really love children and are very patient with them, but the Vansickel children tested *to the limit* the staff of any restaurants we favored with our business. There are some restaurants to which we can never return.

When we finally got home, we would shove Cindy and the children out of the car in their driveway as each child cried and begged to come home with us. By this time I had not enough energy left to feel bad about leaving Cindy with two crying children. Also, by this time, I didn't even like the children.

When we pulled into our garage I would rush in to see how mom had fared while we were gone. While I paid mom's sitter, Courtland would clean the "fishy crackers" and apple juice out of his expensive English car. That was our weekly outing! That was my entire recreational activity for the week!

I should take this time to acknowledge the excellent help I received with mom in the person of Gale Nelezen. Gale had almost died, and God spared her life. She considered the job of helping with mom a ministry, a "thank you" to God for being alive. She was truly "God sent." Mom couldn't speak and I found that without any feedback from her, it was hard for me to talk to her. But Gale talked to her about her family and her pets. She brought some of her pets to visit (including her pet pig). She took mom for outings to the mall, and to her own home. She prepared wonderful food for her. She would choose a good television show that they could watch together. She kept mom and her room clean during the hours she spent with her. I couldn't have made it as long as I did without her help. May God bless her for her sweetness to an old and sick lady.

By the time I decided that I was no longer going to be able to be my mother's primary caregiver, I had an active ulcer; I was not sleeping at night, or if I did sleep, I would awaken with a start and rush into my mother's room mistakenly believing she was trying to call me.

I was too tense to enjoy a romantic hour with my husband, I couldn't push my granddaughter in her swing for a few minutes without picturing my mother lying on the floor of her room unable to get up. I felt as if I were literally tied up in knots all the time.

Looking back, I can see mistakes I made, but the reality is that there were circumstances beyond my control which defeated me. How often I thought with regret of the lovely assisted living facility where mom had lived before I moved her to Texas. There her personal care needs were met as well as recreational needs. When I visited I could be the frosting on the cake. Although I had many responsibilities to her while she lived there, they were not daily responsibilities. Once I became her full-time caregiver, I was too tired to be fun and quickly ran out of creative ideas to entertain an invalid lady.

The bottom line was I was too tired, too stressed, too committed to the needs of the rest of my family. Although Gale was wonderful help, I really needed more of a break than I ever got. Like Judy, in chapter eight, I needed two weeks at a resort hotel.

Living with the "Kids"

NO CHOICE

As I tell this story, I realize that many people have little or no choice about providing care for an elderly parent in their home. In reading Rosalynn Carter's book I was impressed that her mother provided care, first, to a dying husband while still caring for her four children. Then she cared for her father for 25 years, and held down a full-time job. Her story makes me look like a wussie. However, we did have another choice. That was to place mother in a private care facility where she could receive the physical care she needed, and I could return to being a fun daughter who would bring her home for visits and take her for drives, etc.

DEMENTIA

Considering caring for someone with dementia presents an entirely new dimension to the challenge of caring for a parent who is merely unable to perform personal care tasks. The demented parent is able to move about, even leave the house, but at some point can't be trusted to safely use appliances or take a walk. Sometimes a victim of Alzheimer's disease will even be violent.

My friend Ann got a long distance call from her parents' neighbor. The neighbor told Ann that her father had become abusive to her mother. This confirmed what Ann had suspected but her mother had denied. There was no longer any possibility that Ann's mother could care for her husband at home. And Ann didn't feel that keeping the two of them in her home with her father violent and prone to rages was at all practical.

How can I say that bringing a demented parent into your home to live will never be successful? But honestly, that is what I believe. The reality is that a parent with dementia is not a good candidate for home care. None of the people I have talked to who are caring for an elderly parent in their home is attempting to care for a parent with dementia, especially Alzheimer's. What I have found is that many children are attempting to help a mother or father care for the spouse who has dementia. The parent will not institutionalize a spouse with dementia until they have reached the limit of their ability to provide care and decide that for the demented spouse, it no longer matters where they live.

The great tragedy in dementia is that the elderly person loses even the joy of being with their family. The family in turn is caring for a body without the mind of their loved one. Additionally, the caregiver can never be off duty. Persons with dementia may sleep sporadically. They may strongly wish to wander off and may be very cunning in their ability to find ways of escaping from the family home. With caregiving responsibilities so crushing and the realization that the elderly person is not benefiting from being kept at home, the question of what is to be lost and what is to be gained by home care versus institutional care often makes the choice clear.

CONCLUSION

Although caring for a parent in your home is not a measure of your love for the parent, I don't want to sound cynical and indicate that it isn't a loving thing to do. I am sure that Mother Walker loved being in her daughter's home around all the family there. Mother Ellis, if placed in an assisted living home, would have missed seeing her family as much as she did. My own mother loved being in my home and having me tuck her in at night. I just wish I could have continued to keep her in my home.

Additionally, there are certainly times when the cost of placing a parent in a public facility is prohibitive. Or you may live in an area where there is nothing available that you would choose for your parent. In this case I hope the stories told will give you ideas on how to survive being a full-time caregiver. As I mentioned elsewhere, Rosalynn Carter's book on *Helping Yourself Help Others* is a wonderful manual for the caregiver. I would highly recommend it to all caregivers.

I offer these ideas to help those of you who can choose between home care or a commercial residence determine whether you can be a successful full-time caregiver. I suggest you consider the health of the caregiver, the family makeup, the other demands on the caregiver, the support which the caregiver will have, and how much time and energy the parent will require. How tied down to the house will the caregiver be? Is the parent difficult to be with? For instance does the parent complain or nag, or is the parent depressed? The answer to those questions should help you assess the chances of home care being successful.

One reason I offer these cautions is that moving my mother from my home to a personal care facility was a traumatic experience about which I still feel pain. I wish I had never brought her to live with me since I couldn't continue to care for her. It is easier to recognize beforehand that bringing a parent into your home is not workable than to move them out once you have made that choice.

8 When You Are the Enemy

I clipped this letter from the *Los Angeles Times* a few years ago:

> "Dear Abby: I am 67 years old and I am crazy. I got this way taking care of my mother, who is 92. She is positively the most impossible woman who ever lived. Unfortunately, she is in better health than I am. I'd sign this but she'd kill me."

As though being a caregiver is not difficult enough under the best of circumstances, sometimes the parent begins to view the child, who is providing help, as the enemy. This is often the first indication that the parent is suffering from dementia. Anger and suspicion directed toward a child can be caused from things other than dementia, as we will discuss later in the chapter, but very often this is a signal that something is going wrong in the thinking process.

The story of my friend, Judy, and her mother Grace, is typical of how a sweet loving mother can change into an angry and suspicious one. Notice the reaction of Judy's brother. His reaction, too, is classic and totally typical of siblings who may not be the recipient of abuse from the parent.

JUDY'S STORY

Judy and her mother, Grace had always had a good relationship. In fact Grace had moved into a townhouse close to Judy's home so they would be in the same part of town. During the second week of each month, Judy would spend an evening at Grace's house paying bills and balancing the bank statement. It was a good time of combining a visit while doing some paperwork. Years before, Grace had given Judy "Power of Attorney" so Judy could take care of a complicated legal matter regarding some property. This came in handy later.

Two problems arose at about the same time. Grace began hiding some of her bills from Judy. Not the checkbook, but bills. Also, Grace began losing her car whenever she shopped at a large mall nearby. After being called from work several times to help her mother find the car, Judy asked Grace not to shop at that mall unless they could go together. Grace was unwilling to make that change and showed resentment at the suggestion.

Judy had a lot of other pressures in her life at that moment. (Isn't that the way life always goes?) She said that having a sick husband and injured son at home prevented her from giving her full attention to the changes in her mother's behavior. However, from talking with lots of families, I have concluded that the family is *always* slow to recognize the beginnings of dementia.

The third thing that happened was that Grace began accusing her grandson of stealing from her. Ross had just moved to St. Louis to go to college. He seemed eager to be close to his grandmother and tried to be of help to her. When Grace began to accuse Ross of stealing money, Judy didn't know what to think. Although Ross was a nephew, he had grown up in another state with only occasional contacts with the St. Louis family. As Judy explained, "I didn't want to believe he would steal from mother, but didn't think I knew him well enough to say unconditionally that he wouldn't."

Judy was caught in a dilemma. Grace would tell one story and Ross would tell quite a different one.

The fourth thing was that Grace began to be angry all the time with Judy. Not only was Grace verbally abusive but now she began to accuse Judy of taking things.

Judy's brother, Joe, and his family drove over from Kansas City. Judy tried to tell Joe about Grace's behavior, but she could tell he didn't believe her. One evening they were all at Grace's house and Grace accused Judy of taking her metal file box where the important papers were kept. Everyone agreed that Joe's two oldest children would search Grace's house for the box. They found it in a short while but instead of being mollified, Grace became even more angry with Judy.

Judy felt sure, now, that Joe would be able to see for himself how unreasonable Grace had become. She felt sure he would realize there was something wrong with Grace. Instead, knowing the personal stress which Judy had been experiencing, Joe came to the conclusion that there was just normal conflict between the two ladies. He decided that the problem was at least partly Judy's. Joe and his family decided to take Grace home with them for an extended visit.

For the next two weeks, Judy was able to focus on her ill husband and injured son. Then the call came from Joe. They had attempted to keep Grace inside their house because she had begun to wander off in their neighborhood which was unfamiliar to her. When Joe left for work that morning, his wife had locked all the doors. Grace, finding the doors locked, threw a heavy chair through a window. Joe's wife was badly frightened and refused to stay alone in the house with Grace. "Would Judy please come and get Grace *immediately?*"

Joe had taken Grace to be evaluated medically, during her two week stay. The doctors had found nothing wrong. But, knowing that something *was* very wrong, Judy spent that night with her mother in the townhouse. The next day they began a search for suitable living quarters in a supervised facility. Grace couldn't understand why Judy didn't just move in with her so she could continue to live in her town home. Another sign of dementia is unreasonable expectations of the caregiver's ability to "fix" things.

After Grace was moved into the "independent living" level of a facility which provided several levels of care, Judy continued to pick Grace up for church services. One day, as she returned her mother to her new home, Grace refused to get out of the car. In the "discussion" which ensued, Grace bit Judy. With help from the staff, Judy got her mother into her room. From then on there were times when Grace was violent with Judy.

The facility where Grace lived wasn't secure, meaning that the residents could come and go. Grace began to "go" and not find her way back. After a couple of times when she was found in situations which were dangerous, the director said Grace could no longer live there. She recommended that Grace be placed for evaluation in the psychiatric wing of a local hospital. There the doctors were able to determine Grace was suffering from Multi-infarct Dementia. In simple terms, Grace had been having small strokes which were not impairing her physically, but were damaging her mentally. The doctors were able to finally give Judy clear instructions as to how Grace must be cared for, and, of equal importance, they encouraged Judy to get professional counseling.

Worn down by the weeks of caring for Grace and her own family in addition to holding down a full-time job, Judy dearly needed counseling or some kind of emotional support. (What she really needed was a couple of weeks at a resort hotel, but caregivers rarely get to be pampered.)

The anger and suspicion directed towards her from her mother was extremely painful for Judy. Even after she learned that this was due to her mother's mental condition, it still was painful. The words came at her with her mother's voice, from her mother's face. That strong emotional need to be loved by our mother doesn't stop just because mother is ill. Inside, we are still a child looking for mother's love and approval. All of this took its emotional toll on Judy, even as the extra work and energy expended took a physical toll.

Additionally, Judy had lost her mother. The demented lady whom Judy cared for was no longer her mother except, perversely, in her power to inflict pain. So Judy had to go through the grieving process much as though her mother had died. But, heaping insult on injury, Judy still had to take care of an angry, resentful person who laid guilt and pain on Judy. Under many circumstances one can walk away from a relationship which causes so much pain, but the caregiver doesn't have that option. Judy had to find a way to survive the barrage of abuse and complaints.

Judy says that she was with one therapist for one year and most of that time was spent on helping Judy get in touch with her feelings. Then she changed therapists and for six months they focused on Judy's past, her growing up years. Finally she got into a support for "mature women" and their emotional issues. Either because of the previous work Judy had done, or because it was such a wonderful group with a fine leader, Judy experienced real healing from this group.

Judy still cares for her mother. And the things which her mother says still have the power to hurt. But Judy is better equipped now to deal with being perceived as the enemy.

WHEN SIBLINGS WON'T BELIEVE YOU

Judy has forgiven her brother for doubting her when she tried to convince him of their mother's abusive behavior. She remembers that she had doubts about her nephew. Also, she knows how hard it is to accept stories about someone, like a mother, which are so contrary to everything we have ever experienced. She knows that she was fortunate that Joe took Grace home with him and kept her long enough to see for himself that something was very wrong.

Rudyard Kipling has a line in his poem, IF, which expresses the attitude which the sibling receiving the abuse must have toward the siblings who can't accept that there is anything wrong.

> **If you can trust yourself when all men doubt you,**
> **But make allowance for their doubting too;**

NONDEMENTED PARENTS WHO ARE ANGRY

When you feel you are becoming your parent's enemy and you are sure there is no dementia present, you need to look at other causes for the anger.

Anger toward the caregiver can occur as a result of the anger and grief which a parent experiences as they become physically limited. The aging process is often accompanied with loss. What ever that loss is, it is natural for the parent to mourn that loss. In her book *On Death and Dying*, Elisabeth Kübler-Ross, M.D. lists the parts of the grief process. They are denial,

73

anger, bargaining, depression and acceptance. If your parent is in the anger stage of their grief, you may get the fallout from that and be, for a time, their enemy.

Another possible cause you should look at is just how far you have taken your role as caregiver. Are you trying to **parent your parent?** This is something you must never do. You can never be your parent's parent. You must always remain their child.

When Judy read this paragraph, she challenged it. "How can we not 'parent our parents' when they are unable to care for themselves?" she asked.

This is a good question. I will try to explain how I perceive the distinction. The difference in being a **caregiver** to a parent and a **parent** to our young children is found in our objective. Our objective when we are raising our children is to teach and train them. We punish and discipline them. We expect them to change commensurate with their age and development.

We are not responsible for teaching or training our parents. It is improper for us to try to reform or change them. We provide council and care. We become resource people who supply good information so they can make their own decisions. We make sure they have good medical and living conditions. Depending on their mental abilities we may make business decisions for them. We protect them from harming others because of poor driving ability, etc. We protect their assets. We **do not** protect them from knowing about problems in the family.

We will explore ways in which we can **"HONOR"** our parents even in our role as caregivers in another chapter.

SUMMARY

When you become your parent's enemy and dementia is present, your task as their caregiver is increased manyfold. You may have trouble convincing siblings of the problem. They may in fact, side with the parent. Your inner child's need of love and approval from your parent is denied. You experience grief at the "loss" of your loving parent. You may need to resort to legal means to be able to preserve your parents' assets and take care of their personal business. I hope this never happens to you, but if it does, get emotional support like Judy did . . . and send your parent for a lengthy visit with the unconvinced sibling(s).

9 | The Emotional Roller Coaster

Some days you're a bug, some days you're a windshield.
Price Cobb

If you are a caregiver, this is probably the hardest job you have ever done or will ever do. For me it was more difficult both physically and emotionally than raising children, even teenagers. I knew that my children would grow up, grow more independent. As a caregiver to my parents, I knew we were on a downward spiral. Things were not going to get better; my parents would grow more and more dependent. With teenagers you hope each birthday will bring more maturity and you know, as a friend reminded me when our youngest daughter was making us crazy, "She will be forty someday." With parents, at each birthday they are less able to take care of themselves.

I expected to be a caregiver for my children. For some reason I didn't expect to be a caregiver for my parents. I was unprepared either emotionally or intellectually for my role. I was often frustrated when the things I "fixed" came "unfixed" so quickly. I was frightened, unsure, bewildered, and at times resentful. I grieved and went through all the steps of grief; *denial, anger, bargaining, depression* — except the final step, *acceptance.*

With our parents, we aren't sure what our role should be. Most of us spend a lifetime respecting them and listening to them. Stepping into their lives feels impertinent to us and is often very threatening to them. A friend shared how fearful he was of telling his father he could no longer drive. The problem was solved when the insurance company canceled the father's coverage after a minor accident.

In this chapter I will attempt to identify some of the conflicting emotions which the caregiver can have. Perhaps it will help to know you are not alone — that others are experiencing and have experienced the same roller coaster of emotions as you.

CONFUSING EMOTIONS

The range of emotions often seems inappropriate and in conflict. If we have always loved and respected our parents, we are confused and uncomfortable with the feelings of frustration and sometimes rage which we may feel toward them. Our desire to see them well cared for creates anxiety. Watching them fail physically and mentally causes us to grieve and develop fears for our own future.

My friend Joan resented having her retirement years "spoiled" with a clinging mother who put guilt trips on Joan for not spending more time with her. Joan asked, "Why does she expect so much of me? When she was my age she could travel, spend time with her grandchildren and pursue hobbies. But she accuses me of not being a proper daughter if I don't spend all my time with her."

Joan loved her mother and felt guilty for not being with her mother whenever her mother asked, but her mother's need was so great that it cut deeply into Joan's time. Joan wanted to meet her mother's needs but at the same time she wanted to have her own life back. The tension created guilt and resentment at the same time.

The **WORLD** tells us that if we have good parents we should gladly and joyfully help them in their declining years. This shouldn't feel like a burden. By contrast, **GOD** has always allowed his children a full range of emotions. If you doubt this, read the Psalms or Job. It is normal and healthy to have emotions. We just have to remember that our emotions are helpful signals but they aren't road signs. We just can't let our fears and resentments prevent us from doing the task which has been given us.

FEAR

Several years ago I asked twenty-five ladies in a Sunday School class what it was they most feared. I was amazed to learn that what they most feared was growing old and helpless, unable to take care of themselves.

It won't surprise you to learn that these women were generally between forty and sixty years of age. Many of them were caring for their elderly parents. Their fear reflected the losses they were watching their parents experience as aging took its physical and mental toll. They wondered if they were looking into the face of their own futures. They wondered if their children would feel as burdened as they were feeling. They dreaded the time when their own children might feel resentment at having to care for them.

Being a Bible teacher I felt I should be able to present something from Scripture which would calm their fears. I wanted to find a biblical example of a caregiver providing elder care, while skillfully balancing job, marriage, child rearing, etc. Or a great person of God dealing with incontinence or dementia with peaceful acceptance.

There really isn't much in Scripture which deals with being a caregiver or how older people in Bible times dealt with the physical and mental changes brought on by aging. This is a bit puzzling since people seemed to live a long time. Maybe they grew old but just didn't age as we think of aging. After all Sarah at ninety was still so beautiful Abraham was afraid for his life if the local king took a fancy to her. Sarah lived to be a hundred and twenty-seven; did she ever have to wear Depends^{TM}? We just aren't told.

It is recorded that Peter's mother-in-law lived in his home. However, it seems she was in pretty good condition because after Jesus healed her of her fever, she got up and served them tea and crumpets or whatever people served guests in Capernaum. We have no record that she made Peter's nights hideous by getting up at all hours and asking, "Where is my breakfast?"

Scripture records that Isaac lost his eyesight when he grew old. This, however is not a positive story to present about aging since Isaac's blindness gave Rebecca an opportunity to trick him into giving the "eldest son" blessing to Jacob. Additionally, there is no mention of his being a lot of work for Rebecca. I guess she had servants to fetch and carry, take Isaac for walks, etc., otherwise Rebecca would have been too tired to scheme and plot.

Did Lydia's household include elderly parents? If so, did mom wander off during the day while Lydia was at work and get picked up by the police? Was she afraid that her father could no longer safely drive his chariot?

Is it possible that people in Bible times didn't have the problems with aging we are having today? Or else do the writers just fail to mention those little domestic details?

It seems that the Patriarchs did a lot of leaning on their staffs and terrorizing their children. Well, that much hasn't changed. I know a number of elderly parents who terrorize their children.

My parents didn't terrorize me but the things which happened to them as they aged brought fear to my heart. I well understood the fears the ladies in my class were experiencing.

My parents had it pretty rough. Little pieces of their lives kept falling off.

Nineteen years ago my father had a stroke which affected his reasoning ability. He could no longer drive. He couldn't interact socially except with one or two well known people. He had to be reminded to bathe and change his clothes.

One of the first things my brother and I asked the neurologist who diagnosed our father's condition, was, "What about us?" We were thinking, "Will this happen to me? Will I have to give up my independence? Will I become so forgetful that someone must care for me twenty-four hours a day?"

HIDING FROM FEARS

Two unhealthy ways we hide from our fears are by (1) masking our fears with other emotions such as anger or (2) avoiding the parent. I hope I never showed it, but I would experience such rage at my mother when she drooled her food, or when she could no longer use the controls on her television that I wanted to shout at her. I couldn't understand my rage because it was so unreasonable. Then my friend, Marti, a clinical psychologist, asked me if I was seeing myself in my mother's condition. The scales fell from my eyes. It was fear that I was experiencing, but as I often do, I chose to avoid my feelings of fear by substituting anger. (Some of the anger may have been related to my grief.) Of course hiding my fear behind anger only confused me. It was much healthier for me to recognize the emotion I was having was fear and deal with that.

Another manifestation of fear is avoidance. I am convinced that many children who won't help with a parent's care or won't even visit the parent are really avoiding facing their own fears. Men seem to have the most trouble with confronting fear. So it seems we more often see men avoiding their responsibilities to aging parents. If you have a sibling who rarely visits the parent, he/she may be avoiding seeing the parent in a condition which he/she fears being in someday.

HEARTBREAK

It was at 2:00 a.m. in the fall of 1977 when I got a telephone call from the police department in Garden Grove, California. "Is this Anita Johnson? We have your father here. He doesn't seem to know where he lives."

I can't remember my feelings as I made the 20-minute drive. Walking into the police station, I saw my father sitting on a bench along a far wall. He didn't stand up when he saw me come in. He just looked at me and in his eyes I saw bewilderment, fear and *embarrassment*. To me, he had always been the strongest, most resourceful man alive. Seeing him sitting on a bench in a police station like a frightened child waiting to be rescued was one of the worst moments of my life.

The sergeant behind the desk (probably a lovely man) made some kind of joke about people not knowing where they live. I wanted to slap his face! I wanted to shout, "**THIS IS MY FATHER. HE IS THE BRAVEST MAN ALIVE. HE CAN GO ANYWHERE. DO ANYTHING. HE CAN TRACK BEARS IN THE ROCKY MOUNTAINS. HE CAN EXPLORE THE**

JUNGLES OF HONDURAS . . . HE *HAS* DONE THESE THINGS! HOW DARE YOU TELL ME HE DOESN'T KNOW WHERE HE LIVES." The sound you hear is the sound of my heart breaking.

GRIEF

There are many things we grieve over as we watch our parents age. We grieve over the things they lose. We grieve with them as they grieve over their loss of health and independence. We grieve over losing them.

I lost my parents long before they died. My strong doting father was lost to me and in his place was a sweet child. He could no longer bring me silly little presents and hike in the forest with my children.

The mother who loved me and was interested in everything about my life and the lives of my children became a helpless lady who could no longer even talk to me.

I grieved over losing them as grandparents for my children. But I guess the worst was just seeing them deteriorate week by week, month by month, until finally I longed for death to release them from bodies which no longer served them. And, I hope I won't be misunderstood, I longed for the release their deaths would bring to me as their caregiver.

My husband Courtland understood. On the day of my father's memorial service he said to me, "Anita, it is all right for you not to grieve any more. You have done your grieving. It is all right for you to feel relief that your father is no longer imprisoned by a mind and body which no longer serves him. It is not wrong for you to feel you have had a burden lifted which has been heavy and you have carried for a long time."

Some caregivers are devastated and experience feelings of disorientation when the person they have been caring for dies. For others, like me, their death is a release. I didn't shed tears for my father for many months after he died. Then as the memory of his illness faded, I cried over the loss of the daddy who had loved me so much and had been such an example of courage and strength.

For those of you who are caring lovingly for a parent, I would like to give you the permission my husband gave me. If you do not grieve at your parent's death, it is not because you are a "bad" person who didn't properly love your parent. If you feel relief that you no longer have to carry that heavy burden of care, it is not because you are unloving and selfish. If you have been faithful in your task, you may be proud that you did what had to be done to the best of your abilities. That is all anyone can ask of you.

FRUSTRATION

You have a responsibility to help. You must help. But your parent has ideas too, and they aren't used to letting the "kid" make their decisions. As the parent begins to lose the ability to do certain things, they may try to hold on even harder fearing that letting go of any area of their life means slipping into the abyss of helplessness. You make suggestions. They refuse. You present ideas. They don't understand. Either your help is refused or too much help is asked. Just as you think one problem is solved, another pops up. Then the first problem reappears.

My husband Courtland's ninety-year-old father called. It seemed he had some business to take care of but felt unable to manage either physically or mentally. He had not previously asked for any kind of help.

Pleased to be able to help his father, Courtland asked what needed to be done. Dad Johnson said he needed to visit his Savings and Loan Co.; he had a business letter regarding his retirement which he didn't fully understand and some other items which required driving around town.

Courtland was a C.P.A. — paperwork was his specialty. His chest swelled with the anticipation of helping his father and at the same time showing "dad" what the "kid" could do. He said, "Gather up everything you need to take care of, and I will come as soon as I can and help you take care of everything."

We made a lot of calls and cleared Courtland's calendar for the following morning. It wasn't a middle-aged C.P.A. who drove off down the freeway; it was a knight on a white charger riding out to rescue dear old dad from the dragons.

It was a very deflated middle-aged C.P.A who returned a few hours later.

"What is wrong," I asked, "Weren't you able to help your father?"

"Yes, it only took a few minutes. I explained the letter and we reinvested dad's T-bills. When I asked 'what's next?' dad said, 'That's all. We can go home now.' Then when we got home, dad said, 'We will go tomorrow to see my insurance agent.' It seems that dad thinks in terms of doing one errand a day."

"Doesn't your dad realize that you have a busy office and it is difficult for you to get away and that you needed to take care of everything in one morning?" I asked.

"No, he doesn't realize that. And I can't tell him without it seeming that I have no time for him or don't want to help!"

Frustration! Frustration!

AMBIVALENT FEELINGS

I had wonderful parents as I am sure most of you had. But some parents aren't so wonderful. What are the emotions of the adult child whose parents need care but there isn't much love and gratitude for the kind of parent they were? There must be a lot of unresolved anger toward bad parents. Now the parent, who wasn't there for you when you needed them, is on the needing end of the stick. It is easy to imagine that Satan might put it into your heart that this is an opportunity for revenge. Or at the very least neglect.

I have one friend, Sheila, whose feelings aren't a bit ambivalent. Her parents were abusive and made her childhood a living hell. At age fourteen she was "adopted" by a lovely Christian couple. She doesn't anticipate providing any level of elder care to her parents. She has come to this decision partly from the belief that it would not be healthy for her to be around them and partly from the belief that she "owes" them nothing. Her foster parents on the other hand will receive her loving care if they ever need it.

Aside from those parents who were truly wicked people, as were Sheila's, most parents do the best they can. It seems a currently popular belief that all adult problems are related to bad parenting. This is a worldly point of view which has no basis in Scripture. At the risk of sounding terribly simplistic I would suggest that if your parents made some mistakes (and all our parents did), it is probably high time that you forgive them and move on with your life. I would remind you that revenge is never a godly choice. I certainly cannot tell you what level of care you should be providing your parent(s) but this might be a good time to remember that God does not deal with **US** as we deserve. Even if your involvement in your parent's life is limited to the kind of help you would provide a neighbor or a distant relative, I feel confident that after they are gone, you will be glad you gave even that much.

Let me tell you about a Dennis the Menace cartoon I once saw. A little girl was telling Dennis, "Mrs. Wilson doesn't give you cookies because **you** are nice. She gives you cookies because **she** is nice."

Maybe, if your parents were short of perfect, you can find it in your heart to give them care, not because they were nice, but because you are nice.

GUILT

Someone has said, "Guilt is the gift that keeps on giving." Guilt seems a strange emotion for a caregiver to feel. Yet that is an emotion you may expect as a caregiver. How do we feel guilty? Let me list the ways.

No matter what I did for my mother, I was never satisfied. It never seemed enough. Once when I was searching for the "perfect" place for mom to live, my friend, Sue, said to me, "Anita, this is your **mother** you are trying to find a place for; nothing will be *good enough for your mother*."

During the twelve years I provided some level of care for my mother, I was also a wife. I am always amazed that no matter how busy I am, my husband has expectations of me. Just kidding. I knew I had to cherish and care for my marriage, but that too, suffered neglect at times when I was too busy, too tired, too distracted to be a companion, let alone be the fun lady my husband thought he had married.

I am the mother of three adult children. Even adult children sometimes would like to have a mother to spend time with, cook them a holiday meal or remember their birthday. My step-father died on April 19 after months of a lingering illness. Our youngest daughter's 18th birthday was April 20. We had given not one thought to her birthday present or any kind of celebration. Major guilt!

My husband and I had a business. When I was away caring for parents, or on the phone regarding their care, or involved with paying their bills, etc., it was my husband who took up the slack working longer hours doing work I could have been doing.

There wasn't enough of me to go around. Whatever I was doing, something was being left undone. There seemed to be needs everywhere, church, friends, community. It is easy to feel terrible guilt about all you fail to do. I used to wish I could clone myself so that I could be all things to all the people who wanted something from me.

It is common to feel guilt that you can't "fix" a parent's life. It is hard to accept, but the reality is that the caregiver can't restore a parent's lost health or lost mental abilities. The caregiver may not be able to maintain the parent in the parent's own home. We can't replace the lost spouse. We can't provide better television programs. We can't make their friends and family members come visit. Their life will never again, on this earth, be what they would like it to be. That is not your fault, and it is not something you can fix.

SUMMARY

At my mother's memorial service, my friend Susan said to me, "Anita, you have been a faithful daughter." My first reaction was to protest. I had made so many mistakes. I had resented the "interruption" of my own plans. I hadn't always liked caring for mom. I hadn't been able to do and fix all that I had wanted to do and fix. Then I realized that Susan hadn't told me I had done a perfect job, not even a good job. She had told me I had been "faithful." She, the wise lady that she is, concluded that being "faithful" during twelve years of caregiving was good enough. Somehow, I think that for God, "faithful" is good enough. Perhaps for you and me, "faithful" should also be good enough.

10 | "Honor Your Father and Mother"

"I have over 42,000 children, and not one comes to visit."
Mel Brooks as the 2000-Year-Old Man

As our father became increasingly dependent on my brother and me, Gene cautioned, "We must always protect his dignity. We must always treat him with the respect due a parent even though he is childlike in his need to be looked after. He must feel that we are still his 'kids' and he is still the parent." Gene was very good at being sensitive to dad's feelings and his need for respect. What I learned from him, I will share with you. This chapter is dedicated to the memory of Gene Robert Mills, one of the best of all sons and brothers.

DON'T BE BOSSY

Many years ago when my father's family felt my grandmother Mills should no longer live alone, her oldest living son built a "granny flat" onto his house in Florida. Although my grandmother's health was good and her mind sharp as ever, my uncle assumed the role of boss. He has been dead several years now so I can't ask him why he felt he should assume such a role but I recall several things that happened which distressed me. One time grandmother wanted to work at her church's booth at the county fair but uncle refused to "allow" her to do so. She was disappointed but complied with his wishes. Again I am puzzled by the dynamics which dictated that kind of thinking from either of them. Perhaps she believed that accepting his hospitality required her to accede to his wishes. And, perhaps, he believed that he had assumed some kind of responsibility to the family to keep her well and safe. I remember thinking that the decision denied her something which would have given her great pleasure.

Perhaps you, too, have observed this kind of bossy attitude by a caregiver toward a parent. Sometimes any level of involvement by an adult child is perceived as an invitation to "take over" the elderly parent's life and insist that the elderly parent must do as they are told. The motives behind this kind of thinking are unclear. However, one might wonder if there are buried resentments which surface at this time. "Now," thinks the adult child whether consciously or unconsciously, "is my chance to get back for all the unfair treatment I received during my childhood, or to fix all that is wrong in the parent's life which caused the family distress over the last fifty years." Or perhaps the caregiver just mistakenly takes on the role of a parent because of the many tasks they must assume which make them "feel" like they are the parent. Whatever the motives, I wish to caution my readers against this kind of thinking. Even though you are *asked* or *must* become involved in your parent's life, it is important that you remain sensitive to the fact that *you are the child, they are the parent.*

One way in which you can be watchful is by asking yourself if you are doing too much. Are you providing help where help is not needed, asked for, even wanted? A parent who is aging and unable to live alone should still be able to make as many life decisions as they can. A friend who read this chapter said, "Sure, they make the decisions and I have to provide the help for them to do as they want." Let me hasten to explain that this is NOT what I mean. That would be letting a parent become a tyrant rather than providing willing support. Let's give a couple of possible scenarios using the story of my grandmother and my uncle.

If my uncle was concerned about grandmother's physical ability to man a booth, he had a right to express his concern. "Mother, I am afraid that four hours in that booth will tire you too much. Would you be content to volunteer for two hours? Can you work during the cooler evening hours?" Or, if he was concerned about the inconvenience to himself. "Is there someone who can pick you up and later drive you home because I have other plans for my time that day. " Or, "I can drive you but picking you up is a problem; can you make other arrangements to get home?" You see, I am not suggesting that showing respect for a parent must make you, the caregiver, a slave to their wishes. You determine what you are willing to do and be kind but clear about how much help you can/will provide.

RESPECT THEIR RIGHT TO LIVE AS THEY WISH

As mom became increasingly unable to care for her home she was happy to have me come clean her house on Saturday (my day off). My husband put his foot down. He said, "We pay someone to clean our house so you can have Saturday free for other things. It makes no sense for you to spend that day cleaning at your mom's when she, too, is able to pay someone to clean for her." He was right, and I respectfully told mom I wouldn't be able to come and clean again but would be glad to help her find a suitable cleaning lady. Her decision was hard for me to accept. She refused to hire anyone and the house got worse and worse. I had to respect her decision and also had to stand by mine. I didn't nag her about her house. It was **her home** and its degree of cleanliness was her decision. She had the same right to live as she wished at eighty as she had at fifty, or thirty.

ASK IF THEY WANT YOUR HELP

When mom expressed difficulty balancing her checkbook, I offered to do that for her, telling her that I didn't mind doing it. Since this involved a visit with her, she readily agreed.

When she failed to record a check, she didn't need a scold from me on her carelessness any more than I want to be scolded by my C.P.A. husband when I fail to record a check.

Gene and I suggested we be on her checking account so that in the event she became incapacitated, we could access her funds. By putting both of us on her account, she was assured that neither of us would feel "shut out." She was completely comfortable with this.

We need to be reminded that with our parents as with anyone else, when one is in on the decision making, one "owns" the decision and will try harder to make a plan work.

DON'T HIDE FAMILY PROBLEMS
FROM AN ELDERLY PARENT

I cannot say this strongly enough! The most insulting thing we can do to our parent is to hide family problems from them. Unless the parent is suffering from dementia to such a degree that they can no longer comprehend who their family is, they should share common family information, even the painful things.

Children who conceal from a parent anything going on in the family which is unpleasant, often excuse their behavior by saying they are "sparing" their parent worry and pain.

This may well be their motive, but the message the parent will get is that because they have grown old they are no longer considered a part of the family. They are left to guess and wonder at what is really going on. Many times their guess is worse than what is really happening. In one family we know, the wife had gone to Betty Ford for treatment for alcohol abuse. The husband's younger sister brought his mother to visit. He excused his wife's absence by saying she was away on business. Later the mother called her oldest daughter in tears saying she was afraid her daughter-in-law and son had separated. The older daughter said "No, mom, Brenda has gone to Betty Ford's to recover from alcohol addiction." "Oh, thank goodness!" was the mother's relieved response. What she had guessed in the absence of correct information was much more distressing to her than the truth.

The bottom line is that someone who has lived eighty years or so is well able to deal with painful things which happen in all families. And more than that they have every right to know what is going on. Like the mother in this true story, they will know something is wrong and may make a guess far worse then the truth.

I know of one family who is keeping from the mother a

terminal illness which one of her children has. The mother knows something is wrong and that she is being kept in the dark. The only thing the family is accomplishing is to deny her the comfort she would have of sharing with the family their common grief.

The only time I can think of that family would be justified in concealing a family problem would be if the parent is near death.

LET IMPERSONAL AGENCIES DO THE DIRTY WORK

When we finally realized there was something seriously wrong with my father's mind, we knew he should no longer drive. Taking a cue from a friend, we let the insurance agency do our dirty work. They withdrew his car insurance. He was spared the indignity of having one of his children tell him he could no longer drive.

The doctor we took him to for his neurological tests was wonderful. She explained to him as well as to us just what areas of his brain were damaged by his stroke. She was the one who said he could no longer live alone. We got this information as a family, not behind dad's back.

LET THE PARENT DECIDE WHERE TO LIVE

This is assuming that the parent is mentally competent. This worked well with my mother. I tried to present her with all the facts, as I knew them. Then, she always previewed the facilities and approved them before we moved her. Then when we made a mistake, and we made several, it was OUR mistake, not MY mistake. Even a parent who has lost much of her ability to function mentally, can know where she feels at home and welcomed.

Of course this excludes the parent whose level of dementia is bad enough to make asking him to make a decision not only unreasonable but distressing. A parent with dementia, when asked to make a decision, will become anxious. Also, a parent with dementia may not be happy any place he lives. However, whenever practical, an elderly parent should be able to choose his own living quarters.

DECIDE WHICH SIBLING THEY RESPOND TO BEST

Gene and I made a surprising discovery with our father. If we needed to get him to agree to accept a change, he responded better if I was the one to ask. We pondered why this might be true. We knew that he dearly loved and trusted each of us. We finally decided that dad still viewed me as his baby girl. He was not threatened that I might try to control him. Gene, on the other hand, he perceived as a man who, like dad's own father, might try to dominate or control. Making that discovery made the three years we cared for him go much smoother for all. Gene was mature enough to be amused rather than hurt that dad resisted any change coming from him, but for his "little girl" he would do anything.

I have learned that it is common for there to be one child whom the parent(s) are most willing to listen to. I was talking to a friend recently who said that she, of all her parents' four children, was the one whose judgment the parents trusted. One of her brothers is a preacher. All are college graduates and successful people. All are equally loved. Why do her parents trust her most? She doesn't know why, but her advice weighs more with the parents.

GUARD THEIR PRIVACY, PROTECT THEIR DIGNITY

This was an area where my brother was vigilant. Any place where we considered moving dad was carefully screened by him. He would carefully observe how the staff treated the other residents. He made sure that they considered dad's room, **his** room and knocked before entering. He was also beautifully sensitive to dad's feelings. He bent over backwards to treat dad with respect. Dad had always been the first person to reach for the check at a restaurant. Somehow my brother continued to let dad "pick up the check" while protecting him from having to count out his money or his change, neither of which he could comfortably do.

DON'T TRY TO CHANGE THEM

Remember, changing a parent is not your job. You may see lots in their life you want to change. You may have wished for changes in their life for many years. This is not what you are supposed to be doing. If you try, you will make their life miserable as well as your own. I respected my friend, Shirley, when her beer drinking father-in-law came to live with them. She didn't try to correct his drinking habits. As she said, "It isn't my place to reform him." She put beer in the refrigerator and announced to her children, "This is grandpa's beer." She didn't moralize. They were able to draw their own conclusions about the effects of drinking on the human brain.

DISCLAIMER

Please, don't believe that because I have written these things, I was always good at remembering to honor my parents and remain respectful at all times. It is just because I have memories of failing too often to show proper respect that I can write these things with such conviction.

I have related elsewhere that mother lost her ability to use her television remote control. She would get her thumb on the volume control and in a few seconds the entire house would be filled with the sounds of whatever program she was watching. This would be followed shortly by a bellow from my husband who had his office next to mom's room. The first time this happened, I rushed into the room, snatched the controls from mom's hand and brought the volume down to a bearable level. I stood there appalled at my rude behavior. Always after that time I would ask, "May I help you?" And I would wait until mother handed me the control. This is just one example of behavior which I later regretted and from which I want to spare you and your parent.

"Honor Your Father and Mother"

If you can treat your parent with the respect which is due them, if you can remember that you are not the parent and your role is not one of changing or correcting them, if you can protect their privacy and continue to allow them to make as many decisions as they are capable of doing, I promise you will have sweet memories of the caregiving years, and equally important, you will have made their last days far better.

11 | Getting Siblings to Help

> "We must be the worst family in town.
> Maybe we should move to a larger community."
> Bart Simpson (Matt Groening)

Most of us have known or heard about caregivers who were carrying the whole burden of assisting an elderly parent without help from other siblings. In this chapter, I will try to define reasons why some siblings seem unwilling or unable to help "carry the load," as well as methods which may be helpful in getting all siblings involved in helping care for the parents.

First let me say that most caregivers I encounter are working closely and well with other siblings. This was certainly my personal experience. As long as my brother, Gene, was alive, he was a full participant in our parents' care. Likewise, my husband, Courtland, and his sister, Carol have worked together to share caregiving tasks for their parents. The old days when the daughter(s) in the family was expected to do all the caregiving while the son(s) did nothing seem to be largely gone. Maybe the horror stories about sons rarely visiting elderly parents and leaving all the caregiving to their sisters were the rare exception rather than the common practice. Or perhaps the heightened awareness in our society that men can be caregivers to their children has spilled over into an awareness that they can be caregivers to their parents.

There is really no care that a son cannot provide. My brother decided to take mom on a journey from California to Mississippi to visit her good friend who had moved there. On the way, he took her to see some of her cousins whom she hadn't seen in fifty years or more. They traveled in his big Lincoln Town Car, staying at motels which provided special helps for the handicapped guests. He had to assist her with her baths and dressing, but they both managed fine and came home with wonderful stories of their good times. I realize my brother was an exceptional person and that some mothers and sons would not be comfortable with this level of intimacy, but I share this story to illustrate what is *possible*.

POSSIBLE REASONS WHY SIBLINGS DON'T HELP

I asked the director of a retirement facility, Angelica Mead, what she had observed in cases where one sibling provided all the assistance to the elderly parent. Her comment was that she has observed, in some cases, one sibling (perhaps the oldest daughter) takes over in a way which conveys to the rest of the family that she is the only one who knows what must be done and how to do it.

So, if you are a sibling who would like more help than you are getting, ask yourself if you may have sent this kind of message to the other siblings. Are you or have you been critical of their efforts? Do you tell them the gifts they buy for mom or dad are wrong? Do you redo whatever they do? In other words, are you bossy? If you are, you may be denying the entire family a blessing: yourself the blessing of needed help, a sibling the blessing of feeling they are an important part of the parent's life, and the parent the joy of receiving care from all his/her children.

Also, unless all siblings are in on the decisions affecting the parents, they resent being asked to do tasks which they have been assigned and don't agree need doing. I will share with you an example told to me by Ms. Mead.

PAPA DeMARCO

Thirty years ago when Mama died, Papa, who was then only 64 was invited to move into the oldest daughter's home. Thirty years later the oldest daughter's husband retired and the two of them wanted privacy and freedom to travel which having Papa in the house denied them. So, Sister, quite fairly, she thought, asked the oldest brother to take Papa to live with him. The oldest brother said, "No. I never understood why you moved Dad into your house to begin with, but since that was what you wanted to do I said nothing. I won't invite him to live with me. However, I will help you find a good retirement hotel where he can live, and I will help you persuade him to try living there."

Persuading Papa that a move to a retirement home was not tantamount to abandoning him or putting him into an "old folks home" was not an easy task. But older brother, true to his word, hung in there. He brought his father to visit on several occasions until the old gentleman agreed to give living there a try. Sister got cooperation from her brother but just not the kind of help she expected. (Incidentally, Ms. Mead said Papa settled in nicely, made friends, got involved in the activities offered and seemed to thoroughly enjoy his life in the retirement home.)

SONS ARE NOT LIKE DAUGHTERS

Sometimes sisters worry that their brothers are neglecting the parents because they don't go by and visit. In judging brothers for not doing the things sisters do, we make a common mistake — we forget that men are different from women. (Someone has even suggested we come from different planets.) A sister who is expecting her brother to stop by for cozy little chats with mom and dad will probably be disappointed. Most men don't care for cozy little chats. In fact most men would rather have their toenails pulled out by burning tongs than attempt a cozy little chat. However, if she asks the brother to stop by and do a repair job he may willingly do that. Sons are more inclined to visit parents when there can be a focus to the visit, or when others will be there to carry the conversation. My brother and I would often meet for lunch at a restaurant with one of us bringing mom.

IT IS TOO PAINFUL TO VISIT

I mentioned in an earlier chapter, that sometimes sons or any sibling will avoid a parent because they have difficulty dealing with the aging process, illness or dying. If you suspect this may be the case, why don't you ask your sibling if this is their problem. Your question might sound something like this; "David, I know how much you love Dad and how much he enjoys it when you visit him in the nursing home, but I notice you don't often go. Is it hard for you to see him there? Does it just hurt so much you avoid going?" Sometimes, just naming and identifying the problem can help a person change. Of course David may tell you that he just doesn't have time to visit more and you will have to accept that. Trying to put a guilt trip on David will not improve your relationship with him and probably won't get him to visit dad more often.

ARE YOU EXPECTING TOO MUCH?

Realize that your standards of caregiving may be different from your siblings' standards. You may feel that a parent in a nursing home needs a daily visit. I know lots of people who faithfully visit their parent on a daily basis. Other people may feel that once or twice a week is sufficient. You simply cannot expect your siblings to accept your rules regarding what they should be doing. If you are going out of town and want a sibling to visit the parent, simply ask if they can stop by while you are gone. It is not up to you to dictate how often they visit.

THEY MAY NOT KNOW WHAT TO DO OR THAT HELP IS NEEDED

To quote a well known newspaper advice columnist, "Use plain English words unless you communicate better in another language." Nothing succeeds better in these circumstances than good communication. Remembering all that we have said about not imposing your *standards* of help on your siblings, and keeping in mind that men and women have different *styles* of caregiving, and keeping in mind that you must not be *bossy* about who does *what* and *how*, you may need to have some family meetings. Sometimes these meetings are more profitable if just the brothers and sisters are present, not spouses. Courtland, who was very dear to Gene, declined early on to attend our meetings, not because he didn't want to share the caregiving tasks, but as he put it, "It may be easier to arrive at a decision if just the two of you are making the decision. Any task which you want to assign me, I will willingly do."

What these one-on-one meetings did was to bring Gene and me closer together. Six and one-half years separated us in age and we had never grown as close as we did after daddy had his stroke. This blessing was a byproduct of our mutual concern for seeing that dad had good care.

In our meetings we would define what we saw as an existing problem. Then we would discuss solutions. Then we would decide how to divide the tasks which we had agreed must be done. The decisions as to who did what were sometimes based on personal talents, sometimes on personal preferences, sometimes on whose work pressures were heaviest at that moment.

We also agreed that nothing we decided was set in cement. Gene might agree to do a certain task and then call me and say, "Anita, can you do _____ for Dad? I just got a lot of urgent work into my office." (What he would *really* say was, "I'm up to my a_ _ in alligators.") Naturally, I was free to do the same thing if my work load accelerated. We each trusted that the other would pull his load as best he could.

I recently spoke to a man who said his mother was failing physically and still attempting to stay in her own home. I asked him how he planned to support his mother's efforts to remain in her home. His response was, "My sister has just retired and she will take care of everything."

Because I am a rude, pushy dame, I suggested that he was equally responsible to see that his mother was well cared for and that even though his sister was retired it was just possible that she had some fun things planned to do like a voyage up the Amazon, or living in Kenya and studying Swahili. He gave me the most uncomprehending look I have ever experienced. My guess is that he is one of those dinosaurs who thinks it is a woman's job to cook, clean and care for elderly parents.

I don't know his sister. Perhaps she is willing and able to supply all the care mama needs, but if she isn't, she needs to clearly and kindly communicate to brother that she expects that mom's care will be a shared task.

ECONOMIC CONSIDERATIONS FOR THE CARE-GIVER

We met, in Medford, Oregon, a delightful couple who could fill an entire book with their personal experiences caring for elderly parents, two of whom had Alzheimer's. At the time we met them, Jim's sister and her husband had moved into his mother's home to provide care. Jim said his sister's health wasn't good, so he didn't expect she could provide care to the mother for very long, but while she was there, Jim was giving the sister a monthly salary, out of their mother's funds. Here is a man who understands the sacrifice his sister is making and is fair enough to realize that, since she needs the money, she should be paid for her efforts.

I remember reading several years ago (I think in an advice column) about a woman who had taken early retirement in order to care for her elderly parent. She related in her letter that she fully supported her parent who spent nothing toward housing, utilities, food, etc. After the parent died the will excluded her and left everything to a son who had done nothing for the parent.

While I don't think that providing care for a parent is an excuse for the caregiver to "raid" the parent's funds, I think that it makes sense that the primary caregiver be given some kind of monetary consideration if they need and want it. In any money decisions reached by the family members, consideration should be given to the financial position of each family member as well as the funds the parent has. My brother and I were about equal financially. We agreed that mother would pay her way as long as her money lasted. If or when she ran out of money, we would share equally her financial support. If I bought my mother something other than a gift, I used her funds. So did my brother. Neither of us received any payment for her care since our contributions were about equal.

CONCLUSION

To conclude, it is important to ask for help when help is needed. But don't expect help before all siblings have had an opportunity to discuss and agree about what is needed. Sharing the tasks fairly may not mean sharing them equally. Obviously the child or children living closest to the parent may provide more "hands on" help. However, be creative about what siblings living far away can do.

Courtland and Carol have agreed, at least for now, that Mother Johnson will remain in California which means Carol has much more responsibility for Mother Johnson than Courtland. Courtland's much smaller contribution is to manage his mother's money, investing and monitoring her assets. The important thing is that both are content with this arrangement.

If you are a sibling who is carrying a caregiving task alone, you have my sincere sympathy. I know how important it is to receive help and support from your brothers and sisters. When my brother died and I was left alone with mom's care, I deeply missed his help. If you have siblings who just show no interest or willingness to help, I believe you have a right to ask for financial compensation for the time and energy you spend. This may not suit your siblings, and may not be worth the tension it might cause. I'm sure you are aware that there are other and more important compensations for what you are doing than financial ones, not the least of which is the example you are setting your own children.

I will end this chapter with an old Russian proverb:

It seems that the grandfather had grown old and required a lot of care. One day during a blizzard, the father said to his son, "Go out to the barn and get the horse blanket. I will give it to your grandfather and send him out into the storm." Shortly the son returned with the blanket but it had been cut in two.
"Where is the other half of the blanket?" the father asked.
"Oh, I am saving the other half for you when you grow old," the son answered.

12 | Early Signs of Dementia

*I have long thought that the aging process could be
slowed down if it had to work its way through Congress.*
George Bush's gag writers

I am including a chapter on the early signs of dementia
because I think there are several reasons it might be helpful for
a family to spot dementia in the early stages. It can save a lot of
wear and tear on a family who is jumping through hoops trying
to meet the unreasonable expectations of a family member.
Sometimes early detection can slow or reverse the disease.
Many times the person with dementia is in danger of injuring
themselves or others. In my father's case, he should not have
been driving or using a stove to prepare his meals. It may be
necessary to step in and take over the personal business of a
parent/spouse with dementia to protect their assets. We have
friends who had an elderly uncle who had a great deal of
money. The family discovered that the uncle had lost his business judgment and an unscrupulous man had bilked him out of
about $500,000. Once they realized this, they quickly stepped
in and became conservators of his estate. If they hadn't spotted
his dementia, he might have been left penniless. My friend,
Ann, said her first clue that her father was "losing it" was when
the family gathered at a beach resort and she saw that he had
hundreds of dollars in cash lying on the dashboard of his
unlocked car.

I confess to having no professional training to qualify me to
write on dementia. What I offer you comes from four sources:
(1) My own experience with dementia in my father and mother-
in-law, (2) experiences of friends and acquaintances, (3) information supplied by Ms. Mead, a director of a retirement hotel,

and finally (4) information I have gleaned from an excellent book called *The 36-Hour Day*.

The 36-Hour Day explains the term "dementia" as commonly used by doctors as "a loss or impairment of mental powers. . . . Dementia does not mean crazy. . . . Dementia describes a group of symptoms and is not the name of a disease or diseases that cause the symptoms" (p. 6). If you establish that a family member has dementia, I would recommend this very readable book.

CHANGE OF HABITS

Ms. Mead says that clues she and her staff look for are changes in habits. As an example, when a resident who normally sleeps late suddenly begins to awake at the crack of dawn, the staff is alerted to something which might be causing the change. Another symptom would be a resident who is normally sunny and warm who becomes cross and distant.

In cases where a resident has a noticeable change of behavior or habits, Ms. Mead will encourage the resident or a family member to have the doctor check for frequently occurring causes of dementia; an infection somewhere in the body, medications which need changing or the resident may be taking incorrectly (this is a good reason to have the staff administer medications), or depression. These are causes which, when corrected, enable the resident to return to normal.

Ms. Mead said that a bladder infection would frequently cause a perfectly normal lady to go really bonkers. Once the bladder infection cleared up the lady was back to normal. These ladies had not complained of the normal symptoms which younger women experience with a bladder infection, but Ms. Mead was amazed how often she was correct in guessing that was what was causing the symptoms of dementia.

If those three common causes of dementia are ruled out, the family can expect that the doctor should do some routine physical workups and if necessary do a CAT scan and/or MRI.

Ms. Mead also said that one of the things she has experienced in her years as a director has been that a family placing a parent may say the parent has some dementia and then after a short time living in the facility, the parent is alert and functioning normally. She believes this improvement is caused by the better diet and more social stimulation, and the resident is less depressed because of their happier environment. I repeat this information to show that many times dementia is reversible.

STROKE

My father lived alone, so Gene and I didn't have an opportunity to observe his "at home" habits. However, he began to come to our office dirty and unshaven. This should have been a red flag to us because he had always been very clean in his personal habits. Unfortunately we looked for other causes and let a whole winter go by before taking him for a medical checkup. The stroke which impaired his ability to properly care for himself left no physical clues like weakness or paralysis to alert us that he had suffered a stroke. His speech was not slurred nor did he seem changed in any way other than his unclean appearance. Looking back, I can't believe we were not alerted by the change in his appearance. It took a call at 2:00 a.m. from the police station which caused us to realize something was amiss. We later got paperwork from his insurance company which indicated he had been in an automobile accident earlier in the day. He didn't remember the accident. Thankfully no one was injured.

ANXIETY, MISERY, INAPPROPRIATE GRIEF

Mother Johnson began to be very anxious and nervous. It seemed to her that her life had suddenly fallen apart. She wanted Father Johnson and her to move from their home to daughter Carol's lovely guest house near Sonora, California. She complained of back trouble and various ailments which had the doctors mystified. She was grieving over Father Johnson's prostate cancer although Father J. was still well and strong — at 90 years of age as fit as he had been as a kid of 80. Because Father J. *did* have cancer it didn't seem too far fetched that she would be concerned, but her grief seemed excessive in light of his good health. Also, she had recently been struck by a car. Although the checkup at the hospital, including a CAT scan, showed no injury it seemed reasonable that some of her physical complaints as well as her anxiety were appropriate for an 80-year-old who had gone through that sort of trauma.

After the move to Carol's guest house, she was unable to enjoy shopping trips and going out to lunch with her daughter. She grew more and more anxious about Father J. even though he was spending *his* days pruning his newly purchased apple orchard. Our assurances that he might have years of good health didn't soothe her.

There were other indications that she was in the early stages of dementia. Upon receiving an electric blanket for Christmas, she diligently picked all the wiring out of the blanket. She wrapped clothing items in towels and pinned the towels closed before storing them in the closet. Father Johnson watched her carefully while she was cooking to be sure she didn't burn things and that the burners weren't left on. We have all wondered if he didn't realize before the rest of us that something was wrong.

After two years Father Johnson's health did begin to deteriorate and he required nursing care. With an ill husband, no one was surprised that she was anxious and angry. Those emotions are to be expected in this kind of situation. But other symptoms surfaced. She lost her depth perception. A crack in the sidewalk would cause her to grip my arm and slowly and gingerly step across as though she had no idea if the sidewalk on the other side of the crack was inches or feet below where we were standing. That is when I picked up *The Thirty-Six Hour Day*. The loss of depth perception was clearly described as a common symptom in some dementia.

I wish I could tell you that her dementia was reversible, but it was not. MRIs, CAT scans, blood tests, etc. turned up no answers for us. But knowing she had dementia explained many problems she was having which we were futilely trying to correct. We realized her unhappiness with her retirement hotel had its source in her dementia, not in the facility, and we quit moving her from one to another in the hopes she would be satisfied. When she asked to come live with us, we knew she wouldn't be happy in our home any more that she had been in Carol's guest house in one of the loveliest spots in California. We knew that she shouldn't be left alone while we worked ten hours a day. We also knew that her dementia would make her very difficult to live with.

PARANOIA

As the story of Judy and Grace illustrated, paranoia is a common symptom of dementia. Also common is the willingness of family members to explain this paranoia from legitimate causes. When Grace was accusing the grandson of stealing from her, Judy didn't have enough information to label Grace with paranoia. It was when Grace started hiding things from Judy and accusing Judy of taking things, that Judy finally realized something was wrong. As people grow older and less able to cope with some of their business decisions or the complicated world we live in, it seems natural that they may become more fearful, but where excessive paranoia exists, dementia should be suspected.

Often dementia takes lines of personality which are already there and just makes them more pronounced. The person who has always tended to worry will worry even more. The person who is obsessive in some area of their life will become more obsessive. This was one reason Mother J.'s dementia was hard for us to spot. She just became "more so." It is easier to spot symptoms of dementia when there is an opposite change as in my father's lack of personal care.

DEPRESSION

Depression is one of the many signs of dementia which can be caused by other things. It is not uncommon for older people to experience depression. Growing old is a time of loss. Old people lose their spouses and their friends to death. They often lose their driving privileges, their health, energy and their independence. But depression is also a sign of dementia. Make sure your parent gets help for depression, and in the process of treating the depression, dementia may be diagnosed.

FORGETFULNESS, CONFUSION

We all forget things. I, like Grace, have lost my car in the parking lot of a large mall. One time when I lost my car, I decided I might have to remain in the parking lot until the stores closed and the other cars cleared out. (I would have done this rather than admit to my husband what had happened.) But I don't lose my car every week. The difference between normal forgetfulness and forgetfulness caused by dementia is the frequency and finality of the forgetfulness. For the normal brain, the name that can't be recalled will be remembered at a later time. For the person suffering from dementia, the name may never be recalled.

We all experience confusion under some circumstances, especially when we are under stress. With dementia the confusion grows worse. The person may cover for a while, find ways of compensating for and excusing their behavior. Blaming others for their confusion can be a red flag that dementia may be the cause. My mother-in-law was too confused to set her clock radio. She blamed us for not teaching her how even though we had shown her many times.

ANGER

Although anger can certainly have its root in other causes, this is one of the most common symptoms of dementia. People in the early stages of dementia are angry about the things that are going wrong in their lives. They can't find the car keys. They can't remember something important. They lose their way. They can't communicate what they want to communicate. In general, day-to-day tasks are becoming difficult. For some reason they try to hide the fact that their minds are failing. Their frustration and fear comes out in anger. My mother-in-law was angry with us that we weren't "fixing" her life. Grace was angry that Judy wouldn't live with her and help her even though Judy had a home and husband to care for.

110

Early Signs of Dementia

HARD TO SPOT

It probably isn't surprising that families are slow to spot dementia. Certainly no one wants to label a parent as having dementia when the symptoms can be explained by other causes. But being alert to some of the symptoms can prevent a lot of unnecessary problems, allow us to seek medical help sooner and possibly prevent injury or financial losses.

13 Old But Not Impossible

"My health is good; it's my age that's bad."
Roy Acuff at eighty-three

This chapter is addressed specifically to my elderly readers on the kind of parents we need to be when we reach the age when we need some help from our children.

Sally Scott lived until age 96. She was physically and mentally sharp until the day she died. She was my great-grandmother. This is the ending I would write to my own life if I could. This is the ending you would write for yours. The reality is that you and I may come to need some help from our family. If you will permit me, as one who has recently been a caregiver, I will give you some suggestions about how you can best get the help you need without robbing your children of their lives and at the same time retain your independence and freedom to make your own choices.

I will not speak in this chapter about growing old gracefully. Growing old is hard enough without trying to be graceful about it. You have my personal permission to be as ungraceful as you wish. What you don't want to do, however, is to become so difficult to deal with that your family and friends will wash their hands of you, leaving you adrift in a sea of things with which you are less and less able to deal. Nor do you want it on your conscience that providing help to you has left your children's marriages in shambles and their lives and finances in total ruin. Somewhere between your never asking for any help and your asking for totally unreasonable amounts of help is a middle ground that will get you the help you need and save wear and tear on your family.

I believe if you were a reasonably good parent, you have a

right to expect some assistance as you grow older. I believe if you have raised fairly nice children they will be willing, even eager, to provide assistance. Some of the things which will help that happen are (1) good communication, (2) reasonable expectations, and (3) being geographically near family.

GOOD COMMUNICATION

As we become elderly, our children need to know most things about our life from our finances to our health. It may be good manners or good business to be private about our financial situation with friends and neighbors, but it is unwise to keep our children in the dark. It amazes me how many elderly people refuse to reveal their financial situation or ask for help about the best places to invest or save their money. My husband's own parents never asked his advice on where or how to invest their money even though he had clients who paid large fees for his advice. It shouldn't be hard to identify which of our children are good with money or can help with complicated paperwork when we feel unable to cope with those things.

If we trust our children and if they trust each other, it might be wise to put one of them on your checking account, especially if you are a *single* elderly adult. Consider giving one child a power of attorney. Judy's mother had given her power of attorney so she could take care of pesky business matters. When Grace developed dementia, Judy was able to smoothly step in and take care of Grace's financial affairs.

Certainly our children should know about any health problems. As we grow older, if they live close enough, they may need to go with us to the doctor's office to listen to his instructions and ask questions. Unless you tape record these sessions, you are sure to miss much that the doctor says, and you are sure to forget things you need to tell him. I know I forget at age sixty-two. I'm sure at eighty-two I will forget even more.

I wonder if some older parents won't ask for help or advice because they fear that the children will somehow "take over" their life. Again, this is where good communication comes into play. You need to communicate to your children what kind of help you would appreciate and, if necessary, gently remind them that you are not asking them to take over your life. Also, asking for advice does not mean that you have to do precisely as they suggest. My son has a lot of knowledge about nutrition. I frequently ask his advice. However, I have not given up meat and dairy products to live on tofu and Miso, nor does he expect me to. Good decision making requires being able to consider a lot of options and choosing the one that seems right for you.

BE REASONABLE

I often hear stories from adult children about elderly parents who take an extreme course in either maintaining their independence or expecting their children to do everything they want done.

My friend, Beth, visited her independent, ninety-year-old grandmother and found her standing on the back of a chair leaned against the wall of the house, reaching with a rake to knock a ball out of the tree. This sweet lady illustrates the extreme of an elderly person who refuses to ask for *any* help.

At the other extreme are parents who refuses to modify their lifestyle as they grow older and who ask their children to do *everything* they want done. They expect their children to maintain them as their life has always been. It has been my experience that adult children will deny their parents almost nothing. So, if we make unreasonable demands, they will tear their lives apart to try to meet those demands. We must not forget as we grow older that our adult children have lives, jobs, spouses, children, and ministries at church which require their time and energy.

As we grow older we need to consider ways of scaling back on activities we enjoy. That means, for instance, that we might use stores and services nearer our home. We might have a small garden plot rather than the huge garden we once cared for. With some creative thinking we can probably still do many things we once did, just on a smaller scale. One elderly lady I know continues to invite people to her home. Once she was a stunning hostess. Now she serves meals which don't tax her strength and she serves simply from her breakfast bar. She has even been know to "order in" pizza. Her parties are still fun because she knows that a good party is having people who enjoy themselves and a relaxed hostess. Because she invites people over, they remember to invite her. She doesn't need her children to meet her social needs. If we can afford to, we can pay to have something done rather than call on our children.

If we hide things from our children, if we refuse needed help or if we go to the other extreme and expect them to meet our every wish, we will rob them of their own lives during our last years. My mother used to say, "You can ride a good horse to death." You can use your children up with unnecessary things until they have no energy left for things you truly need of them.

GEOGRAPHICALLY NEAR

It may be wise to move nearer your children. This decision depends a great deal on what kind of assistance you need, how often your children can visit you, or you them, and the amount and kind of assistance you can obtain in your own community.

Moving from your home and your community can be very traumatic, I know. But sometimes it is the sensible thing to do. I am acquainted with two ladies who last year made that choice.

Sibyl: When Sibyl was widowed three years ago, she was living in her husband's hometown. Although she loved his family, she decided to move to the city where her only child lived. When I talked to her, she was very happy she had made the move. She loved her church, had made new friends and was thrilled to be near her daughter and her family. The move was not motivated by any health problems; she just decided that she would be happier nearer her daughter.

Amy: Amy was having some health problems. Although Houston had been her home all her life and she had friends and some family there, when the daughter in Austin offered to build a guest house for her to live in, she accepted. There were two inducements: the daughter, Ann, is a pharmacist and since Amy takes a lot of medication, Ann suggested she would like to monitor her medications. Also, Amy liked the security of living practically under the same roof with Ann. Amy had to give up a lot in making the move. She left the home where she had spent most of her life, and she moved away from her church and longtime friends. I asked her if she missed her friends. She said, "Yes, but I am still able to get back to Houston frequently to see them. I am a *flexible* person; that is why making the move has been good."

What she lost by making the move, she gained by the peace she has of being looked after by her daughter. Amy still drives her car. She has found a church where she is already active, and she has made new friends. She tells me that her daughter encourages her to go and do whatever she is able to do. Perhaps she can continue this way until the end of her life.

An interesting thing is that she and the daughter have discussed various scenarios should her health deteriorate. The daughter has said she doesn't plan to personally provide nursing care for her mother should that become necessary. I think it shows a very healthy relationship that these things are freely discussed. They are preventing misunderstandings and disappointment later on by laying the groundwork now. It is healthy that the daughter realizes she is unwilling or unable to give up her job to provide her mother with nursing care, and it is healthy that Amy does not expect her to do so.

GOD IS STILL ACTIVE IN OUR LIFE

**For this God is our God for ever and ever;
he will be our guide even to the end.
Psalm 48:14 NIV**

Growing old certainly can have some rewards. It also can be very challenging. Sometimes the very sweetest, best people experience health problems which rob them of their minds or force them to give up the things which they enjoy. From our limited point of view there isn't any rhyme or reason for who gets good health to the very end or who, like my parents, have major health problems. I remember feeling that God had somehow let my stepfather, Felix, down when He allowed him to spend his last weeks with little mind and in constant pain. Felix had preached the gospel for fifty years. It seemed he deserved a better ending to his life.

I remember praying, during the time I was caring for my father, that my children would never have the work and worry over me that I was experiencing with my father. As soon as the words left my mouth, I repented of that request. I realized that God has lessons for us to learn, and perhaps He would want my children to stretch their muscles, grow closer to each other, or any other of the many lessons the caregiver can learn.

God is not finished with you. Whatever your condition, he can continue to transform you in His image. He can teach, through you, lessons to all whose lives you touch. Perhaps the greatest lesson we can all learn from the problems which come with old age, is the reminder that this world is not our home. We aren't meant to live in this fallen world forever. We need to let go of our love for this world and the things of this world and turn our faces to the life which will be ours in the New Jerusalem.

If you become a prisoner in a body which no longer serves you, remember what the Israelites who were prisoners would say — **"Next year in Jerusalem . . . ."**

14 Of Death and Victory

"So we fix our eyes not on what is seen,
but on what is unseen.
For what is seen is temporary,
but what is unseen is eternal." — Paul
2 Corinthians 4:18 NIV

As I have spoken with caregivers, I have become aware of some who are intensely focused on keeping a parent alive. They won't let mother live alone because she might set fire to her house and burn to death. Dad can't go ice fishing because he might catch a chill and die. It seems that the terror of the parent's death permeates all decisions regarding where and how the parent lives. I believe that in order to allow parents to live their last years (months, weeks) as richly as possible, we must first come to terms with our own death and then with the inevitability of our parents' deaths. Additionally a discussion of death can be a healthy way of freeing a parent from some concerns they may have as well as helping them make necessary preparations and giving their family guidelines about what decisions to make under certain circumstances.

There is no way I can adequately deal with the subject of death in one chapter. I could not do the subject justice even if I devoted an entire book to it; I don't feel qualified to do so. But I will share with you some of my own family's experiences and some things I have learned along the way.

Before we can come to terms with our parent's death, we must come to terms with our own. As believers, one would expect that we would be prepared for and not be fearful of our death, but, truthfully, many of us refuse to think about our death. We push it into some dark recess of our minds as something too fearful to contemplate. Sometimes our parents have fallen into the same trap.

Here is a test you can take to help determine whether you have come to terms with your death. (1) Have you prepared a will? (2) Have you discussed with your spouse or grown children things which they may need to know if you die? (3) Have you prepared a Living Will or discussed your wishes regarding being kept alive with heroic medical measures if you are so ill or injured that recovery is judged impossible? (4) Do you have any positive images of life after death? This test should give you a clue of how much you have come to terms with death.

I remember several years ago, my friend Bonnie was urging me to take Zinc or some other mineral which she said would strengthen my heart. My reply was, "I don't want to take something to **strengthen** my heart, I want to take something which will **weaken** it so it won't outlast my brain."

At the time this conversation took place my father was lying in a nursing home almost mindless and I was longing for death to release him from the prison his body had become.

I had come to terms with my own death and no longer viewed death as a fearsome experience but instead a necessary progression from this world into the next. Thus I was able to view my father's death in the same positive way. I can't emphasize how important this is. Without a healthy view of our own death and the death of our parent, we will not only fail to prepare for the inevitable, but will make the kinds of mistakes which I have been trying to help my readers avoid. I will use an example.

At age eighty, my grandmother had a tricky heart valve. She needed emergency medical treatment when the valve got stuck or she would die. She wanted to go with my family on a trip which would take us through some isolated country. If we took her and she had an attack before we reached our destination, she would probably die before we could get emergency help for her. But she dearly wanted to go. She knew the risk to her life, but she preferred that risk to staying home. Our decision was to take her.

A friend asked me, "How will you feel if you take your grandmother and she has an attack and dies?" This was a good question. I had to think a minute and then replied, "I will feel better about her dying on a trip which is bringing her pleasure than I can deal with having her die at home knowing that she really wanted to be with us."

The point I want to emphasize is that an elderly person with a clear mind must be allowed to make their own decisions about their life. I believed that grandmother had the right to make her own choice. This, to me, is "honoring our parents."

I ask you to make the same contrasting pictures. If you have a parent who wishes to live one way with a certain risk but you want to keep them safe, ask how you can best "honor your parent."

OPENING UP THE SUBJECT

Once you have come to terms with your own death you will be better equipped to talk with your parent about their death. Several years ago I heard a Christian doctor speak on the subject of growing old. She made a valid point. Prepare spiritually and legally for your death so that when the time comes for you to die, that is all you will have to do . . . die!

A few years ago, my mother handed me a hymnbook and asked me to sing one of the hymns for her. I don't sight read music very well, nor is my voice particularly good, so I was puzzled by her request. However, as I sang the hymn, I became aware of the topic. The hymn was about death and what life will be like after death. It occurred to me that mom might want to talk about death. I asked her what she imagined it would be like to be in Paradise. As it turned out, she had lots of questions. This gave us the opportunity to discuss the few Bible passages which would give us clues about what happens when we die. I was able to share what I imagined it would be like for the saved in Paradise.

Let me share with you what I shared with her:

Jesus promised the thief on the cross that, "Today, you will be with me in paradise." Another reference we have is in the story of Lazarus and the rich man, told in Luke 16:19-31. The story says that Lazarus was in Abraham's bosom. What a nifty picture this is. The poor beggar was reclining at a table by the patriarch of the Jewish nation. This gives us a picture of a time and place where there will be no class distinctions. By contrast, in this world, most of us would never dream of approaching some famous, important person. We would fear they would resent our plebeian presence. If, by some unlikely chance, we were invited to a dinner party where some world famous person was in attendance, we would never expect to be seated at their table! But in Paradise, the beggar is dining with the father of his nation!

I find it exciting to think of that wonderful party our Father God invites us to share with Him. What a guest list! The people at that party will be the saved of every generation. There is no "head table," no group of people whom we will feel too shy to approach. The beggar in Jesus' story was talking with *Abraham!* We can talk with him too. Can you imagine anything more fun than being able to ask all the questions which have come up all the years we have been reading the Bible?

Mom and I talked about the questions we wanted to ask. We wanted to get the "woman's" perspective on a number of things. How did Sarah feel when Abraham told her that he had sold the house, bought a tent, and they were going to take off camping for an undisclosed length of time, destined for he knew not where? How did Mrs. Noah feel about her husband spending all that time building a boat, and once on the Ark, what did they do with all that manure?

Mother and I were able to laugh together about some of the things we wanted to ask when we see those people whose lives were recorded in Scripture. She decided she would like to meet Tabitha since mother, too, had made many garments for people. From that beginning, it was a natural time to discuss her wishes regarding many things.

We cannot assume that because our parent has not discussed her death, growing old or health problems, that she has not been thinking about these things. It seems strange but true that some of the most important things we must deal with are sometimes the hardest things to talk about. I once asked my mother if she was afraid of dying. She replied that she wasn't exactly afraid to die but didn't look forward to it. That response while she was still able to enjoy many of the good things of this life was a completely healthy one. However, I believe that a parent who is or has lost most or all the joys of living on this earth is also demonstrating a healthy response when she, like brother Paul, shifts her focus to that life we have beyond the grave. At the end of her life, I believe my mother made the choice to die.

Shortly before my mother died, she was eating and drinking only sparsely. I took her to her doctor, who said that she was becoming dehydrated. I asked about the possibility of putting her in a hospital where she could be fed intravenously. The doctor looked at us intently and asked, "Are you sure you want to do that?" In unison, my mother and I answered, "No!" As Job says, there are worse things than death. With that knowledge we should be able to make better decisions about just what we are prepared to do to preserve life.

My poetess friend, Freda Fullerton, expressed my mother's attitude toward death in a beautiful poem she wrote for my mother's memorial service. The last stanza is as follows:

SO I'VE LEFT THIS HOUSE BEHIND ME
WITH ITS ACHES AND ITS DECAY,
AND I'VE GONE TO SEEK A HOUSE IMMORTAL,
IN THAT LAND OF ENDLESS DAY.
Freda Fullerton, December 6, 1994

Establishing what a parent's attitude is about his own death and his wishes about life support systems is only the first, though perhaps the most important, step. Next, we all need to make a living will and sign a durable power of attorney for health decisions. Filling out these forms encourages parents and children to discuss many topics related to death and dying which may never have been discussed. I repeat, don't be afraid to bring up illness, mental incompetence, and death to an elderly parent. If they haven't talked about such things, you can be sure they have thought of them.

My stepfather, Felix Tarbet, was the first of my parents to die. He had been ill with kidney failure and on dialysis for some time. Finally his condition worsened. He had to be hospitalized. His sweet nature turned morose and sour. He was suffering dementia caused by renal failure. His death was inevitable but could be held at bay for several months if dialysis was continued. The staff at the hospital asked if we wanted to continue to subject him to painful medical treatments so he could live a few more months in the hospital.

Knowing he was experiencing some dementia we weren't comfortable asking him to make the decision. And he and my mother had never discussed such an eventuality. This was a hideous decision for mother to make alone. How we all wished the two of them had talked about what their wishes were under various circumstances. Mother knew that the decision to stop the dialysis treatments should include the Tarbet family. She sent for Felix's only son, Max. Max summed up his father's deep faith as well as his own in one statement, "When we remember what is waiting for him (Felix) in eternity, why would we want to keep him here any longer?"

Max, my husband and I sat with Felix the next few hours as he slipped into a coma and finally breathed his last. At one point I was reading in the Gospel of John. I had a question regarding what I was reading. As I looked into the sweet face of my stepfather, I reflected that if I could ask him, he would know the answer to my question. Then I realized that soon he could be talking face-to-face with that great Apostle. For the first time, it became clear to me just what an exciting journey for the believer death can be. That moment was the beginning of a peaceful contemplation of my own death.

I hope this chapter will help put into perspective just what a caregiver should do. First, to respect the wishes of the parent even when there is a possibility of death. Second, to make an opportunity to talk with the parent regarding death so that any fears can be resolved. Third, to encourage a parent who has not already done so to prepare a will, a Living Will and make his or her wishes known regarding prolonging life under various circumstances. Fourth, accept that you cannot keep your parent from dying. Just let him or her live as richly as possible to the very last.

15 | Bits and Pieces

> "Everything is funny as long as it's
> happening to somebody else."
> Will Rogers

I offer you, in this chapter, bits and pieces of things which you may find helpful as you care for elderly parents. Money and finances will receive some attention as well as cost-saving ideas. Other things I will touch on are health and recreation.

STEWARDSHIP

There are three aspects of stewardship. One is the idea of making the best use of the parent's funds while providing the best care available. Another is our own personal integrity in handling a parent's funds. And finally, our integrity regarding the use of government help like Medicare and Medicaid.

Unless your family is very wealthy, there is usually a concern about some of the high costs of elder care. Wise is the parent who saved during the years of plenty for the lean years which were to come. Both my parents and my husband's parents were "working people." They never earned large amounts of money. We are very grateful to them, however, that they were thrifty and saved part of their income for their old age. They also hoped to leave something to their children, as I believe most parents do. I will say more about that later.

Get the most for your money. There are economies which can be utilized which cost nothing in terms of comfort but can preserve assets. Some of you may be shocked at this suggestion, but I frequently shopped for mother's clothes at thrift stores. Once she could no longer go shopping and try on clothes, I would buy and bring her items she needed. If I spent $1.00 on a blouse and it didn't fit I could give it away without feeling I had wasted mom's money. Both my parents changed sizes several times during their final years. An entirely new wardrobe could be purchased from the Assistance League for a fraction of the cost of new clothing. I promise you they never looked shabby. I took pride in making sure they were well dressed.

If you have a parent living in a nursing home, things may disappear. Usually, I suspect, because of patients who are confused about what is theirs. If you want a "drop dead" outfit for the holidays, birthdays or other times when your family gathers, keep that outfit at home and then bring it in the morning you are going to take the parent out or else re-dress her when you get her home.

I shopped for mom's bras from a catalogue called "One Hanes Place." (They are not paying me to say this.) I began doing this because of the variety of bra styles I could find in that catalogue, but I also saved a few bucks.

I found that through the AARP Pharmacy service, I could save on protective underwear. Additionally, a savings can be made on most medications taken regularly. You just have to plan ahead and order before the parent's medication is gone.

Medicare and Medicaid. At one of the retirement hotels I discovered that a podiatrist was scheduled on a regular basis to cut mother's toenails. This doctor had showed up at her door and offered to perform this task without any cost to mom. Naturally she agreed. I was aghast! I told the director of the retirement facility that I would assume responsibility for cutting mom's toenails. She reminded me that this service was costing mom nothing; **Medicare was paying**. I asked her who she thought was paying for Medicare? I cannot say that this director was getting some kind of kickback from the doctor by scheduling 50 to 100 patients for him to see for a few minutes once a month and bill Medicare "heaven knows what," but I can see this could be a profitable enterprise. Even without our elected officials looking closely at our entitlement programs, I believe it is our duty to responsibly use Medicare. For the person who has no family to check their feet and clip their toenails, one might make a case for having an expensive doctor show up once a month to perform that task, but for someone with a family it seems a very unnecessary expense.

It is a good idea to keep an eye on the condition of a parent's feet, especially if he has diabetes or poor circulation. I put a note on my calendar to clip mom's toenails around the first of the month. Additionally, I pumiced rough places and painted her toenails. I felt I owed her extra service for knocking her out of a visit with a cute doctor.

Making money grow. Mom was lucky to have a son-in-law, Courtland, who knows more than the average person about money and financial planning. His goal for mom's money was to invest in the highest yield, lowest risk places possible. He utilized short-term bond funds, treasury bills, and high interest money market funds. We kept very little in her personal checking account. After my brother's death when I was the only remaining heir, he suggested that we might merge our checking accounts to simplify bookkeeping. I asked that we not. I liked the idea that when I wrote a check for mom's expenses, I was reminded that, **"this is her money."** I never wanted to begin thinking of her money as my money or her expenses as coming out of my pocket. I took pleasure in reminding her that she was paying her own way.

Cashing in on assets. One asset which may be overlooked is the parent's paid-for home. If she plans to remain in her own home, but her income is inadequate, the home can pay for her remaining there. One way is to share the home with some suitable person. We talked about shared housing in order to provide company and surveillance, but it is also a way of generating income. Another way to cash in on this asset is a Reverse Mortgage. The Loan Company appraises the home and agrees to a price, say $80,000. Then they pay the homeowner so much a month while she lives there. When the home owner dies, the home is sold (or the heirs have the option to pay off the mortgage) and the note is paid off plus the agreed-upon interest. If the homeowner can't live in her home at some point, she can rent or sell. Your C.P.A. or financial advisor should be able to explain this option to you.

Inheritance. I believe that when a child begins to think of a parent's money as their own, it is an easy step to thinking of preserving that money for one's own use rather than providing generously for what the parent needs. In line with this I want to state that SSI is for those persons who were unable to provide for their old age or who have used up their funds. I believe it is dishonest to deliberately give away a parent's funds so they can receive assistance from Medicaid. I recently heard a very sad story from a nice family who told me what they had done without realizing how improper I believe their actions to be.

Go Broke. It seems that grandmother was having some health problems. The family took her to the doctor. While there, they had a discussion about grandmother living alone. The *doctor* told the family they should have grandmother get rid of everything of value because if she had to have nursing care, "*They will take everything she has.*"

The grandmother then gave away her meager savings and her home to her children. She moved across the state to live with her son and his wife. The son and his wife, after the first few weeks, discovered they really didn't like having grandmother live with them. And grandmother, her health improved, didn't like living with them, either. She missed her friends, her church and the activities she now felt like doing. She wanted to go home, but her daughter and five children were living in the house which had been her home. The money she had given her children was used up. Grandmother cannot receive assistance from Medicaid for, possibly, as long as five years because that is how far back her records can be checked to see if she has disbursed her funds for the purpose of qualifying for Medicaid. Which is, in fact, what she did. Meanwhile she has no home and no money to rent even an apartment. I know this sounds like a made-up story, but I promise you this is what one of the family members told me.

I don't think the family meant to be dishonest, but in fact they were trying to get public funds when they weren't entitled to them. In the process, the grandmother was poorly served.

I know that it is hard to see the money a parent has saved over a lifetime being spent so rapidly for nursing care. This is happening in our family, too. It is doubly hard when one parent is still alive and will not have these funds to use. I have a good friend whose father is in a nursing home, and she hates to see how fast his and her mother's estate is being used up. She knows her mother will be left with only a fraction of what the parents had accumulated. However, there are provisions made to protect a certain amount of a couple's funds for the well spouse and still receive Medicaid to help with nursing home costs. This family believes that their Christian commitment requires they not try to hide or give away the parent's funds in order to get help sooner.

Outings and Vacations. For a parent who is able to enjoy outings and vacations, good planning and a little luck can make these enjoyable for everyone. Good planning can mean springing for an expensive lightweight wheelchair. Medicare will not pay for the expensive model, at least they wouldn't for us. However, we decided it was worth the cost. Not only did the smaller chair fit mom better, it was easier for her to maneuver. Not having to lift a big heavy chair in and out of my car trunk made taking her places much easier for me.

One place I often took mom was to a playground. It was a fun place for her, and the added bonus was I could take grandson, Nathan, so I was getting two visits for the price of one. I suggest you try to do things you can both enjoy. A drive is nice. A visit to the zoo is a possibility. Many places have great facilities for handicapped.

The three of us, Courtland, Gene and I took mom to Vermont to visit our son, Mark. We rented a car in Boston so mom could see a bit of New England. One place we took her was to the Peabody Museum in Salem, Massachusetts. We pulled up at the curb in front of the Museum because at this time mom was using a walker. As I began to help her out, a guard from the museum rushed out with a wheelchair. He helped me get mom into the chair and pointed Gene to a preferred parking place. Mom rode through that wonderful museum with its priceless objects from all the places the Captains of Salem took their ships. We all had a wonderful time, thanks in part to the convenience of the wheelchair which the museum provided.

Airlines are equipped to assist the handicapped. Mom and I flew to Texas seated in seats which permitted me good movement so I could help her. I was even able to help her use the tiny bathroom, although I found *that* a bit of a challenge. They helped us on and off, and we got to ride on one of those little cars right to our gate and again to the baggage area when we arrived.

HEALTH

Finding a good doctor is a must. The doctor does not have to be a gerontology specialist but that might be nice. If your parent has a family doctor who seems able to continue with him, that is great. If you use more than one doctor, make sure each one knows about all medications prescribed. I understand that the biggest mistake made in medical care for elderly people is over medication. I kept my own file on mom and when we moved, in addition to having her files sent to the new doctor, I had my own file of information. I suggest you have one sibling always present when the parent visits the doctor. Write everything down.

I can't relate to the stories we sometimes read about patients' wishes being ignored regarding life support systems. The doctors we worked with understood what both my parents' wishes were, were in agreement, and we had no difficulty whatsoever.

Helpful items. A walk through a well stocked medical supply store will turn up a lot of useful items which can make life easier for an invalid and their caregivers. I suggest a waterproof pad on their mattress. Elderly, ill people sometimes have accidents. I placed one on mom's bed under her cotton mattress pad. With her sheet on top of that she had two layers of padding between her and the rubber pad which we were warned tended to be drying to elderly skin. Disposable pads are a good idea to keep on hand. After dad's stroke he took a nap in my back bedroom one Christmas. When he awoke he was wet. A waterproof pad on the bed with a blanket over it would not have hurt his feelings. I just hadn't realized what declining health can do to an elderly person.

After many T.I.A.'s mom had trouble swallowing. Liquids were a particular challenge for her. Through a nursing home we discovered a product which thickened the liquid without changing the taste. It is called "Thick-It." If your pharmacist has problems locating where to order, call 1-800-333-0003. This is a non-prescription product.

Incontinence. A parent who has been in a nursing home for a while will sometimes be incontinent. This is often because the staff is too busy to help patients use the bathroom. If the parent is unable to get to the bathroom herself, the staff may put her in diapers. After leaving the nursing home, her bladder can be retrained. Mom's doctor instructed me to take her to the bathroom every two hours during the day. In a day or two she was back to normal. The diapers which some nursing homes use are very hard on an elderly person's skin because they are airtight. There should be a regular time when they can air out or they will get horrendous diaper rash.

There are many different types of protective undergarments. The style with button-on elastic were our personal favorite. Mom needed some protection but continued to use the bathroom. With the elastic style, she could pull the "paper underwear" up and down, and they were not airtight so she never had any skin problems with them.

Occupational therapist. One lengthy visit or several shorter visits by an occupational therapist can be helpful for the elderly parent who is experiencing loss of mobility or balance. The therapist who worked with mom showed her ways of compensating for weakness in addition to the safest ways of doing things. Additionally, she cautioned me that I was doing too much for mom. She reminded me that mother needed to be doing as much as possible for herself. This was money well spent.

I hope you have found some useful information in this chapter.

16 Boulders in the Path

> "Submit to God and be at peace with him."
> Job 22:21

Many years ago Courtland, Cindy and I backpacked up into the Sierra Nevada Mountains along the Kings River. Our final destination was a high plateau where we could fish and rest before making the journey back down. There were a number of surprises on our trip. Early on we realized that our backpacks were far too heavy. In our inexperience we had packed many things which were unnecessary for our survival. The "trail" we were following was blocked by boulders and trees which had been brought down the mountainside after one of the worst winters the Sierras had seen in years. At one point we had to cross a steep icy place with rocks and a cold rushing river to welcome us if we lost our balance and fell. Before we reached our destination, we were running low on food, we were discouraged and weary. We turned back without ever seeing that lovely, high meadow which had been promised us.

Many poets have used a "path" or a "journey" as a metaphor of our lives. Robert Frost saw it as a path through the woods. I like that image because as we travel a path through the woods, we often cannot see what is up ahead. The path twists and bends leading us we know not where. What we can see, however, is the destination. There is a city set on a hill. In it is the throne of God around which the saved of every generation join their voices in a mighty chorus of praise.

If you are taken by surprise, as I was, by becoming a caregiver, it might help to remember that this is where your path has taken you. Somehow, as with all the challenges we face in our lives, you must do whatever task is given you without losing sight of where you are going.

What I have wanted to accomplish by sharing the things which I have written in this book is to give you some kind of manual you can refer to as you assume a challenging task. I have tried to warn you of some of the mistakes which can be made. I have tried to open you up to creative options and solutions. I have attempted to shed some humor on the situation.

Finally, I want to give you permission to make your own decisions regardless of what others are doing or expect you to do. Your family is unique. Your situation is unique. With love and much prayer you can blaze your own path through this particular bit of forest.

The compass I would give you is as follows: Keep your balance. Get rid of the extra weight. Keep your sense of humor.

KEEP YOUR BALANCE

You cannot do everything. You cannot fix everything. You may not be able to meet all your parents' expectations. Their requests may be reasonable or they may not be. With their own needs so urgent, they may lose sight of the reality that you have other demands on your time and energy.

A Call in the Night. In the wee hours one morning Mother Johnson called from her retirement hotel. She told Courtland that she was dying and he should come immediately. Her voice sounded strong, so he wasn't too alarmed. He called the front desk of the residence and asked one of the ladies there to check on her and call him back. Shortly he got a call saying Mother Johnson seemed fine. The lady on duty had invited her to come to the front lobby where there was a pot of coffee and some cookies. The ladies on the night shift were visiting with each other between tasks they had to perform during the evening. They would include Mother Johnson in their chats and keep her company.

She refused to join them, and as soon as Courtland hung up the phone Mother Johnson called again, this time angrily asking why he hadn't come. He responded that he would visit her after work the next day but meanwhile he needed his sleep.

He reminded her that there was a staff of people to look after her. A few minutes later the phone rang again. When Courtland answered, no one said anything. He hung up and the phone rang again. Several times this happened. Finally he got up, dressed and drove the ten minutes to the retirement hotel. He went to his mother's room, unplugged her phone and pointed out the emergency cord she could pull if she became really ill and needed a staff person to come. Then he came home and went to bed.

At the breakfast table the next morning, he was the very picture of wretched guilt. "I unplugged my mother's phone." The statement hung there to be considered in amazement and guilt.

It took an impartial bystander to point out that his mother's request was unreasonable and his actions weren't mean but the actions of a reasonable man. His mother was all right; her realistic needs were being met. Her wish that he should provide her company in the middle of the night was not the expectation of a reasonable mind.

Keep your balance. Do the loving things, do the important things, but be reasonable about what you try to do or you will destroy yourself long before your parent stops needing you.

GET RID OF EXTRA WEIGHT

When I unloaded my backpack after our trip, I found a transistor radio among other items which added unnecessary weight. There are times in life when we are carrying around a lot of unnecessary weight. Probably **most** of our lives we carry around a lot of unnecessary weight. What is it the writer of the Hebrew letter said? ". . . let us throw off everything that hinders." Good advice for the path of life even when we are not hiking in the Sierras or taking care of elderly parents.

How many things do we do that are unnecessary? I can't remember who, but I once heard someone say, "Ask, . . . does it need to be done and does it need to be done by me?" There are two times in your life it is especially important to ask those questions — when you are caring for toddlers and when you are providing elder care.

Boulders in the Path

You may no longer be able to keep the pantry stocked at your church. You may decide not to hold an office in your home owners association. You may not take your turn teaching the newcomers class. Your ministry at this point is mom and/or dad. You have done your part and will again do your part, but maybe just for a while you will have to let go of some jobs.

Another extra weight you don't need is the expectation of others. You cannot let others decide for you what your role in your parent's life is. It seems there are "standards" we are all supposed to follow. (1) If your parent is in a nursing home, you must visit every day. (2) You must let mom or dad live with you. (3) If you are the daughter, you have more responsibilities than your brother(s). (4) You must do everything yourself; you can't expect your parent to pay for services which you can perform. If you buy into these "standards" or any others which others impose, you are setting yourself up for burnout. Do what you feel right doing. If you have the time and wish to visit the nursing home each day, by all means, do so. If not, visit as often as you comfortably can and ignore the critics.

Needless to say, the writer of Hebrews was talking about ridding ourselves of the weight of sin in our lives. At any time in our lives when we are facing major challenges, the healthier our spiritual lives are, the stronger our anchor is, the better we will be able to meet those challenges. Be sure to carve out time for prayer and Bible reading. I found the Psalms wonderful comfort.

KEEP YOUR SENSE OF HUMOR

At the beginning of our hiking trail, we had to pass through a boggy area which was the capital of the mosquito kingdom. They came at us, babies, old folks, seasoned warriors, and bit us through our clothes and on every inch of exposed skin. We had to pass through the same area on our way back to our car. This time we were better prepared and sprayed ourselves liberally with Off™ and made a dash through. As we emerged from the boggy area, we met a family taking a short hike. The father of the family had on the smallest little blue bathing trunks I have

136

ever seen, and he had the whitest skin. I could hear Courtland suck in his breath as he pictured this man and his sweet children in the mosquito bog. He mustered up his last remaining strength and said, "The mosquitoes get pretty bad up ahead."

The father just laughed and said, "We'll outrun them."

A few minutes later we reached the parking lot where we had left our car. We pried the backpack straps out of the grooves they had worn into our shoulders and flung them on the ground. Then we too rolled on the ground laughing as we built a picture of what had happened when that nearly naked man hit the mosquitoes. We decided that if we had the energy to go back up the trail we would find a blue bathing suit and a body sucked entirely dry of blood. The laughter and the promise of a hamburger and fries were wonderfully restorative.

We all take the burdens of this life too seriously. We get bogged down and forget that we can have fun and laugh at ourselves. If we can't laugh at ourselves, we'd better find something else to laugh at. As Solomon wrote, laughter is good for us. Rent a funny movie, read an Erma Bombeck book, go to the park and watch children play.

Step back and look at yourself from another perspective. Do you have a smile on your face. Can you take time to smell the roses? When I let myself get so enmeshed in caregiving that I could no longer have any fun, I was in burnout.

I believe that joining a group of other caregivers can be one of the most helpful things you can do. You will find you are not alone, and hearing other caregivers tell their stories will provide you the laughter and sometime the tears you will need to get you through.

VAYA CON DIOS

I have attempted to write a guilt-free book which will help you through a difficult time. I know from experience that you can survive. Your marriage can survive. You may have a few more wrinkles and gray hairs, but you will survive.

I also know from experience that you will be glad for having provided loving care for your parent. You will look back with a sense of accomplishment. When someone compliments me on the care I gave my parents, I feel proud that I did what had to be done as well as I could. The added bonus is that, hopefully, I have been able to share some things that will help others traveling the same path, encountering the same obstacles.

You, like me, may struggle with being *accepting* of some of the challenges which you find along the paths of life. During the last three years of mother's life, I kept on my nightstand along with my Bible, a wonderful book by Henry Gariepy called *Portraits of Perseverance: 100 Meditations from the Book of Job.* In it I discovered a wonderful quote which seemed to speak directly to me. I share it with you.

Only in acceptance lies peace not in resignation nor in busyness.

Resignation is surrender to fate.

Acceptance is surrender to God.

Resignation lies down quietly in an empty universe.

Acceptance rises up to meet the God who fills that universe with purpose and destiny.

Resignation says "I can't."

Acceptance says, "God can!"

Resignation says, "It's all over for me."

Acceptance asks, "Now that I am here, what's next, Lord?"

Resignation says, "What a waste."

Acceptance asks, "In what redemptive way will You use this mess, Lord?" (Quoted in *Lord if I Ever Needed You*, Creath Davis, Baker).

When our path takes us to the challenge of caring for our aging parents, we need to remember that we are where God has placed us. Like the boulders in our path, a challenge doesn't prevent us from continuing on our journey. We just have to find healthy, creative ways of dealing with the boulders. We can survive this challenge with sanity and faith intact if we keep our balance, lighten our load and keep our sense of humor.

Remember you are not alone on your journey. "Emmanuel" is the promise that God is with us. Eventually we will reach that lovely, high meadow with the river full of fish where we can feast and rest.

About the Author

Anita Johnson is better known as a speaker than a writer. She admits that her writing is a new adventure for her. In addition to this book, her articles have appeared in *ALIVE* and *Daughters of the King*.

She was prompted to write this book because this was the book she needed during the fifteen years she provided varying levels of support and care for her father and then her mother.

This book reveals her gift as a storyteller. Each chapter takes the reader into the lives of the elderly and their caregivers. There are practical helps and ideas as well as warnings about what not to do.

A mother of three and grandmother of two, she and her husband, a retired C.P.A., have always been involved with family and church. Their ministries have usually sprung from the needs they saw in their own families. Most recently they developed a Single Parents class for their church. Previously they have done seminars on money management.

They live in the Texas Hill Country where they have developed what she calls a family compound so they can be near the two grandchildren and their single-again daughter.

Anita is an active member of the Austin Christian Writers Guild.